LONG
Long

RED
Red

HAIR
Hair

LONG

RED

HAIR

MEAGS FITZGERALD

CONUNDRUM PRESS

First English Edition   Printed by Gauvin Press in Gatineau, Quebec, Canada

Library and Archives Canada Cataloguing in Publication

Fitzgerald, Meags, 1987- , author
          Long Red Hair / Meags Fitzgerald.

ISBN 978-1-894994-95-8 (paperback)

1. Fitzgerald, Meags, 1987- --Childhood and youth-- Comic books, strips, etc.
2. Bisexual youth-- Canada--Biography--Comic books, strips, etc.
3. Witches--Comic books, strips, etc.
4. Redheads-- Comic books, strips, etc.
5. Graphic novels. I. Title.

HQ74.43. F58A3 2015   306.76'5092   C2015-903869-3

Conundrum Press, Greenwich, NS, Canada   www.conundrumpress.com

Conundrum Press acknowledges the financial support of the Canada Council for the Arts and the Government of Canada through the Canada Book Fund toward its publishing activities.

Canada Council   Conseil des Arts
for the Arts   du Canada

For my mom,
a small but
fierce woman.

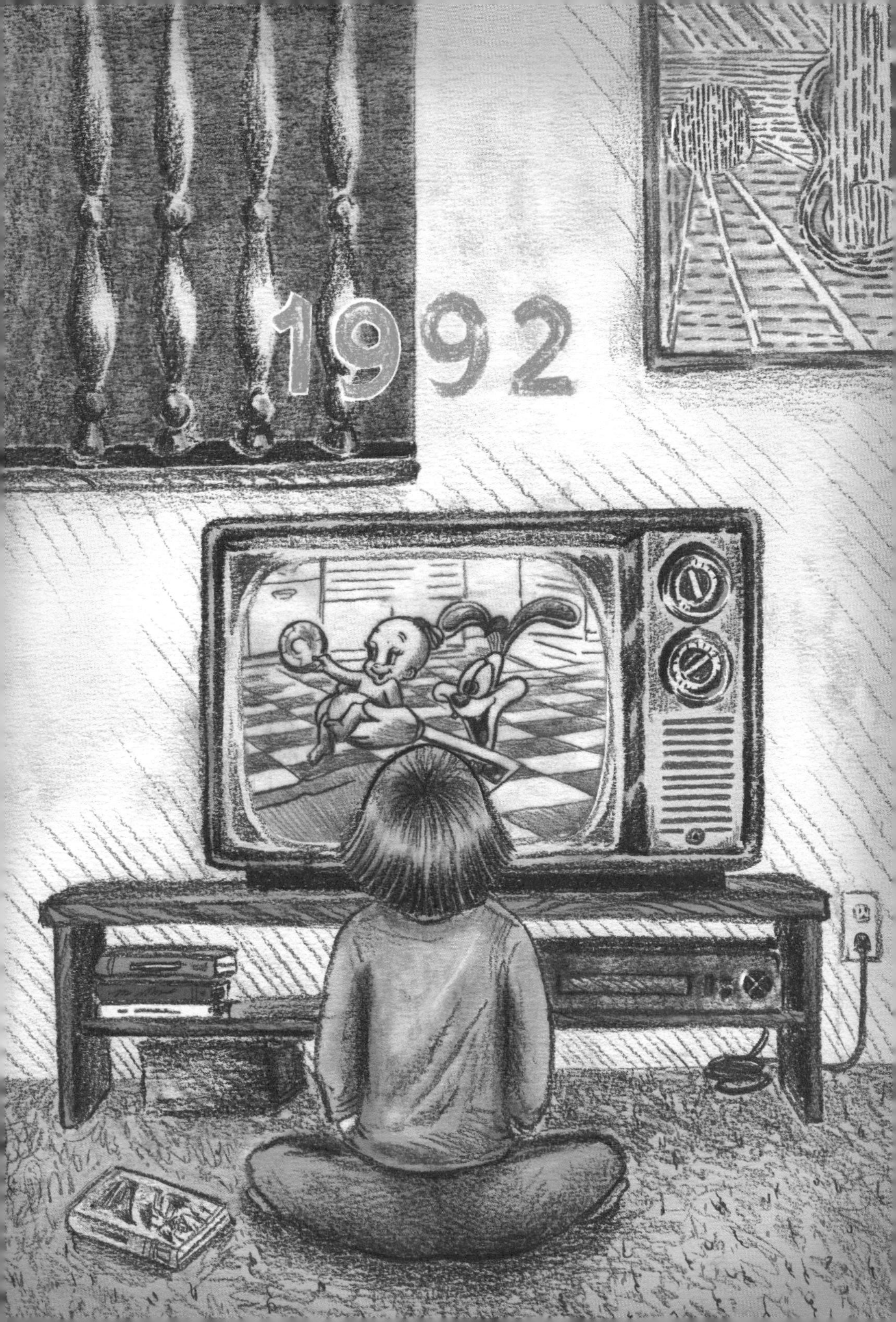
1992

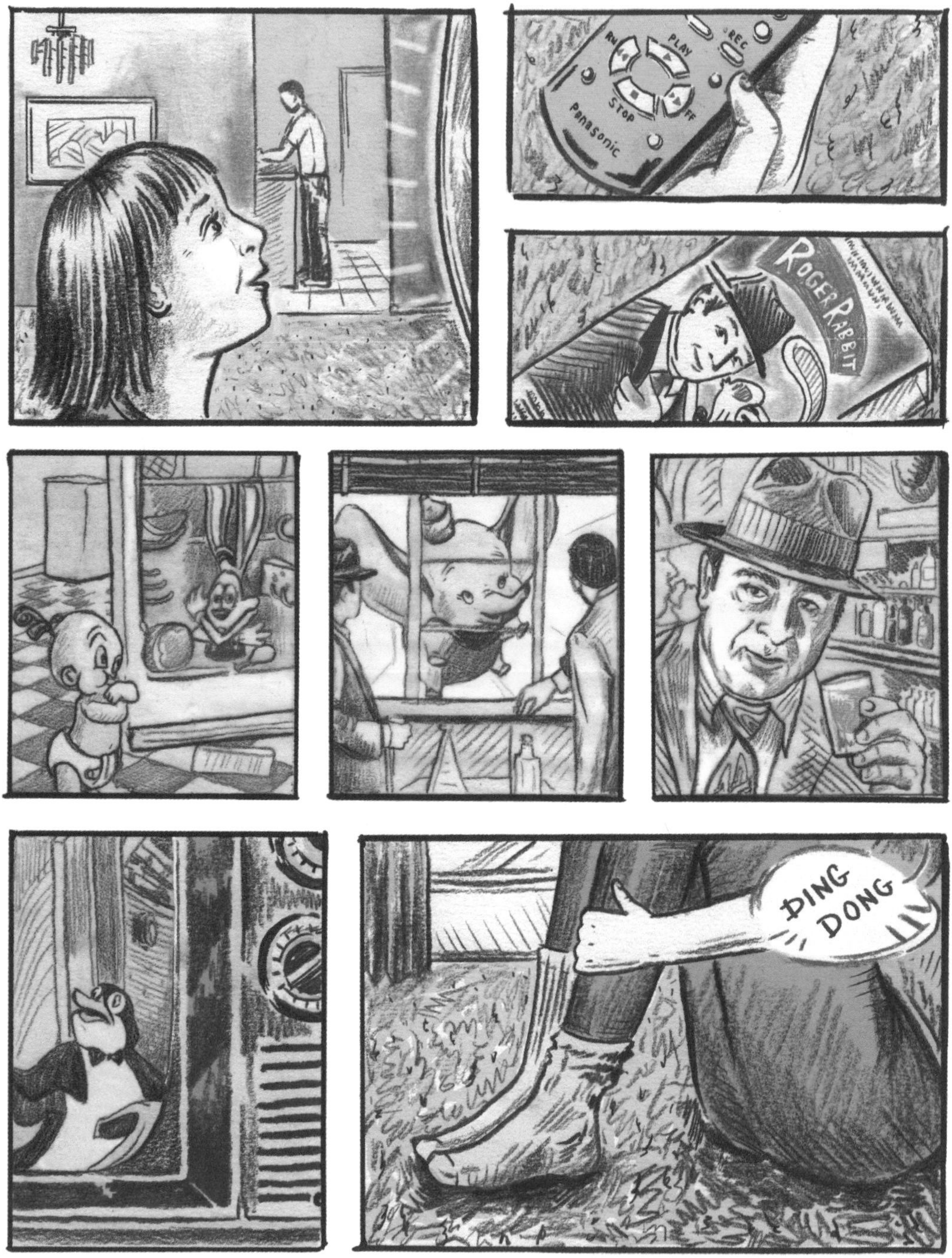
RW
PLAY
REC
STOP
FF
Panasonic
ROGER RABBIT
DING DONG

I WAS AN INTROVERTED CHILD, NATURALLY SUSPECT OF MOST MEN AND ESPECIALLY UNCOMFORTABLE AROUND THOSE THAT I WASN'T RELATED TO.

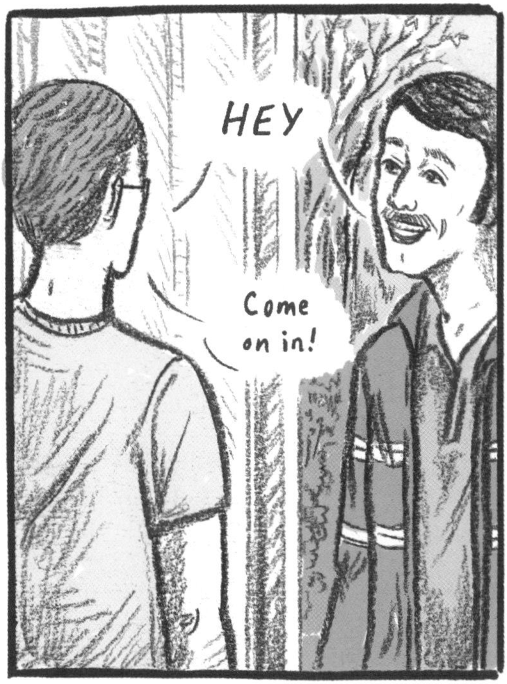
HEY
Come on in!

ERIK WASN'T MY REAL UNCLE,
US KIDS JUST CALLED HIM THAT.

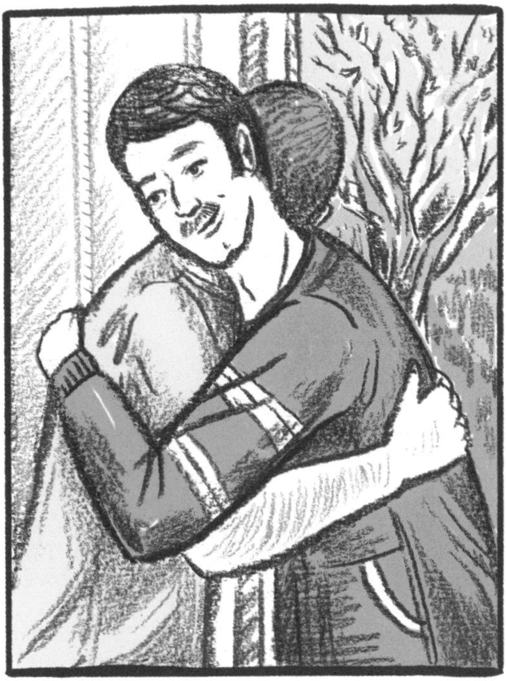

HE WAS ONE OF MY DAD'S BEST
FRIENDS FROM HIGH SCHOOL.

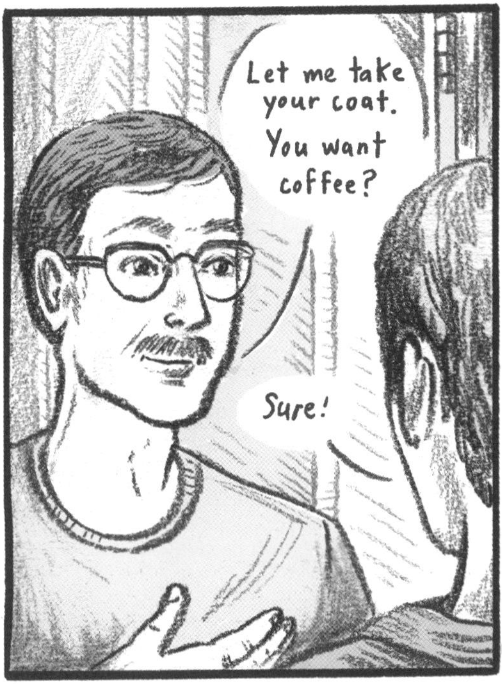
Let me take your coat. You want coffee?
Sure!

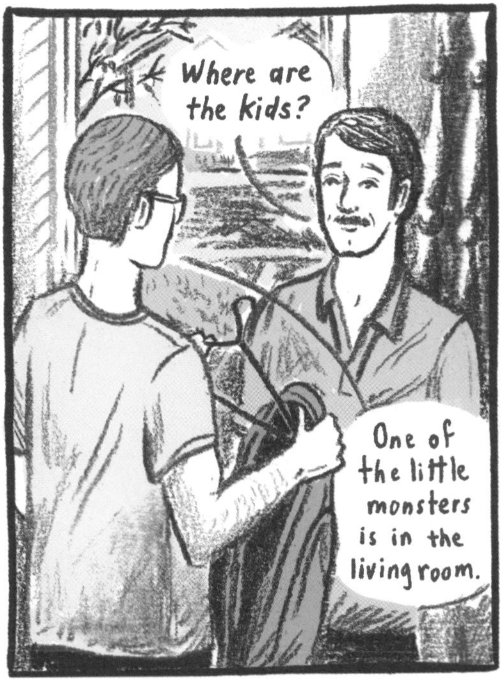
Where are the kids?
One of the little monsters is in the living room.

Hey there!

Hi Uncle Erik

I DIDN'T FEEL WEIRD AROUND ERIK.

I GUESS I JUST KNEW THERE WAS NOTHING TO FEEL WEIRD ABOUT.

What are you watching?

The Roger Rabbit movie.

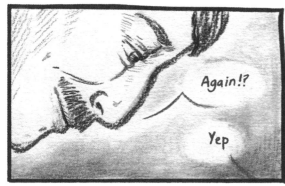

Again!?

Yep

can I watch with you?

Yep

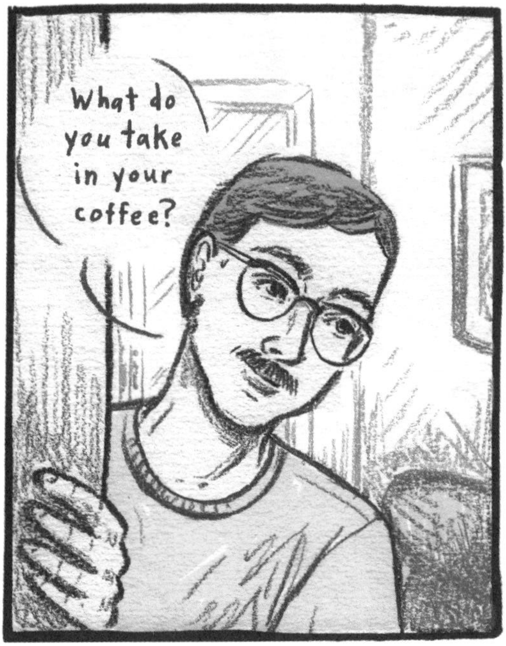
What do you take in your coffee?

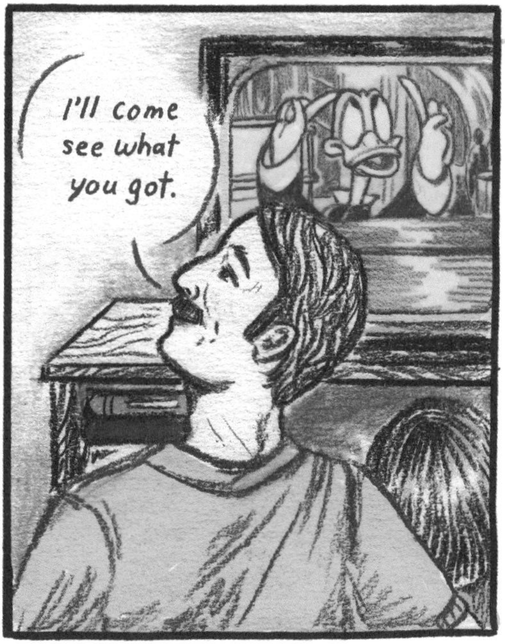
I'll come see what you got.

NO ONE HAD EVER EXPLAINED HOMOSEXUALITY TO ME, BUT I HAD SOME UNDERSTANDING OF HOW ERIK WAS DIFFERENT FROM OTHER MEN I HAD MET, EVEN AT THAT AGE.

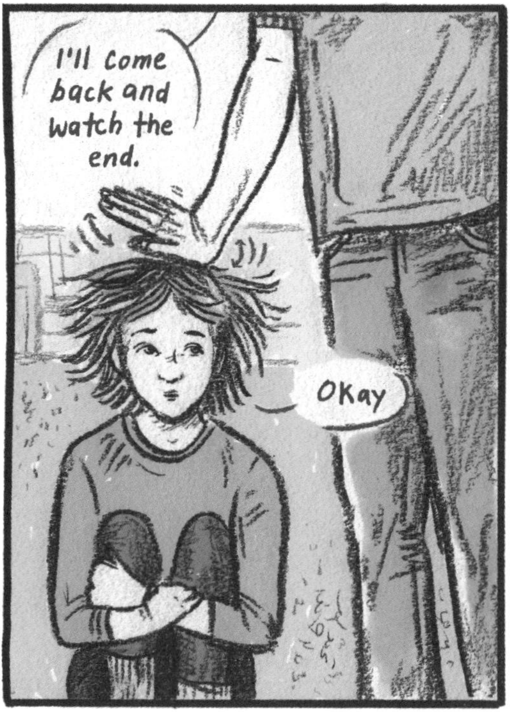
I'll come back and watch the end.
Okay

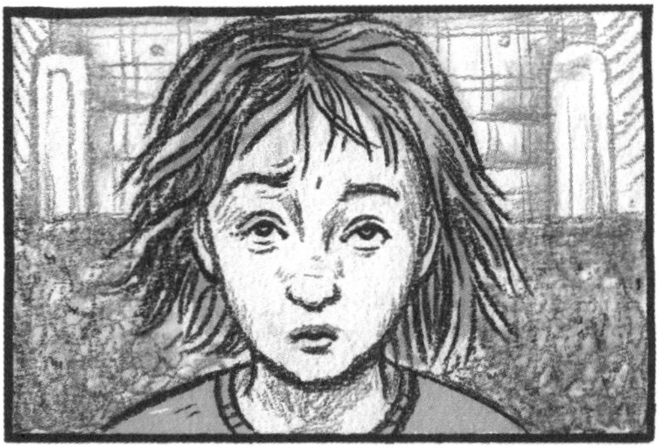

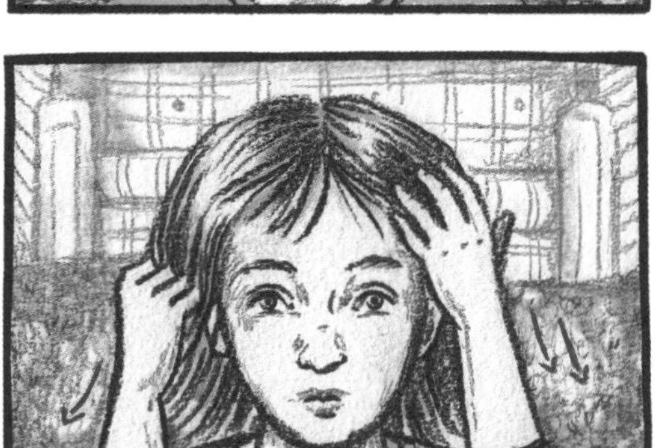

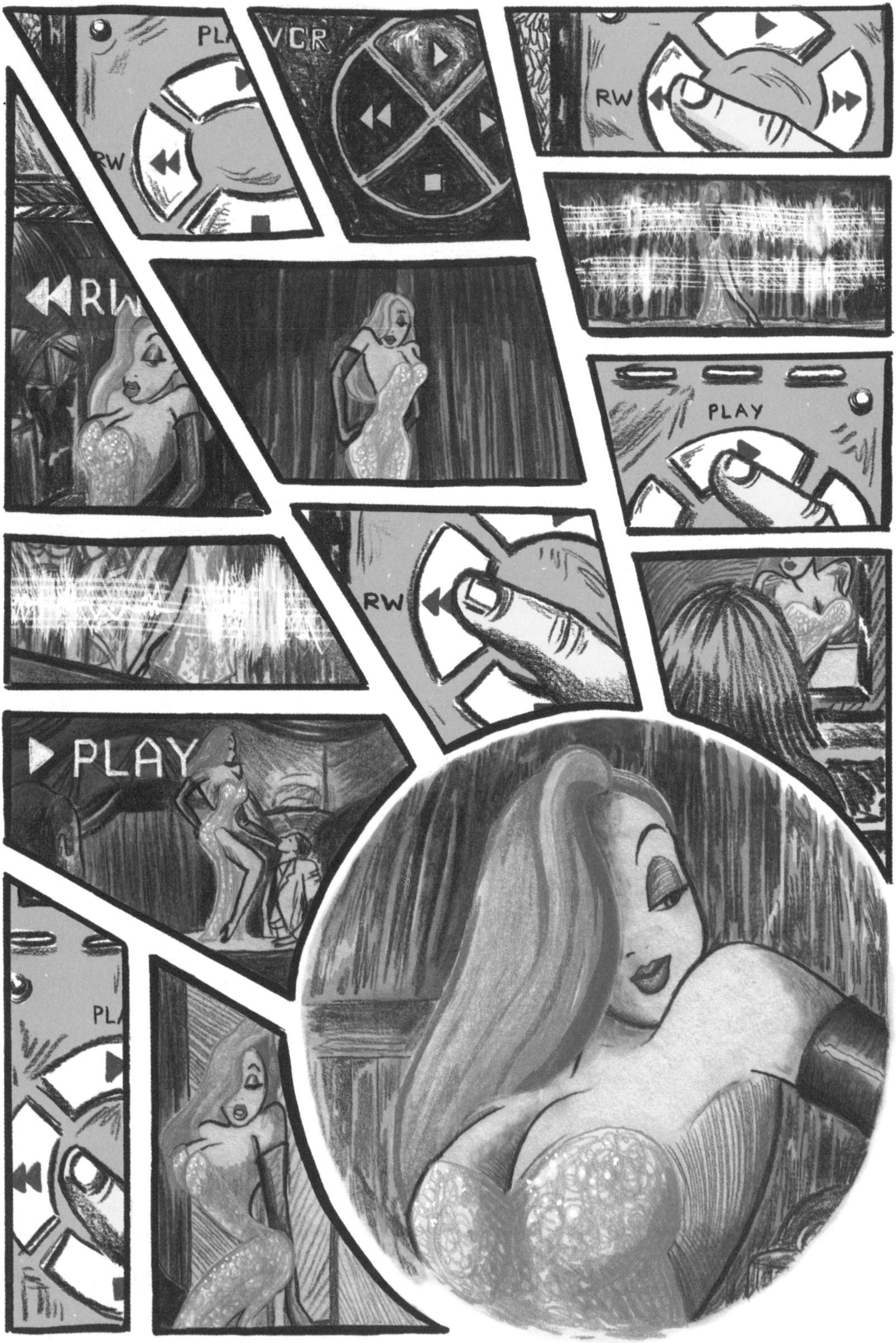

PLA
VCR
RW
RW
RW
PLAY
RW
PLAY
PLA

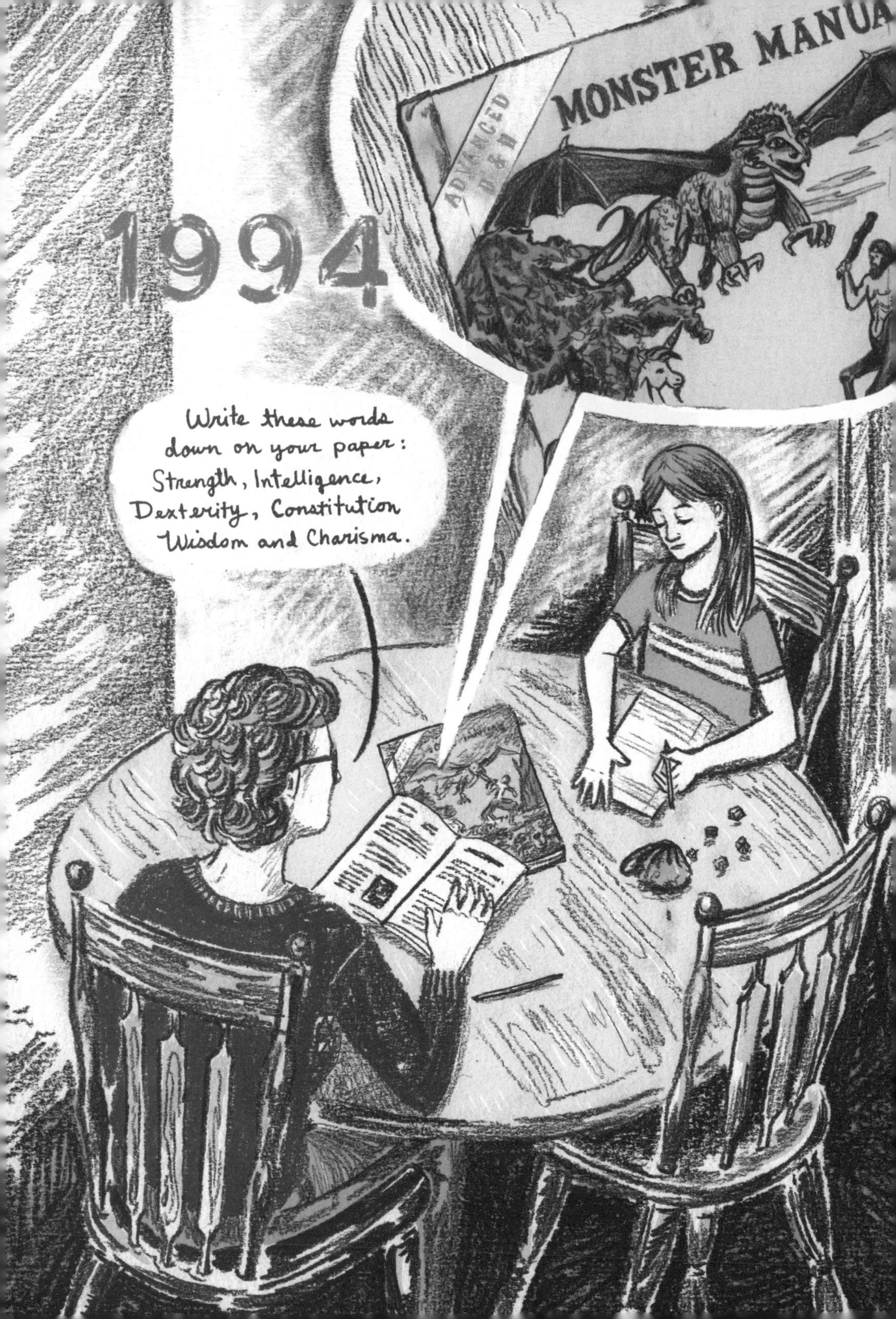
1994
ADVANCED D&D
MONSTER MANUA
Write these words down on your paper: Strength, Intelligence, Dexterity, Constitution Wisdom and Charisma.

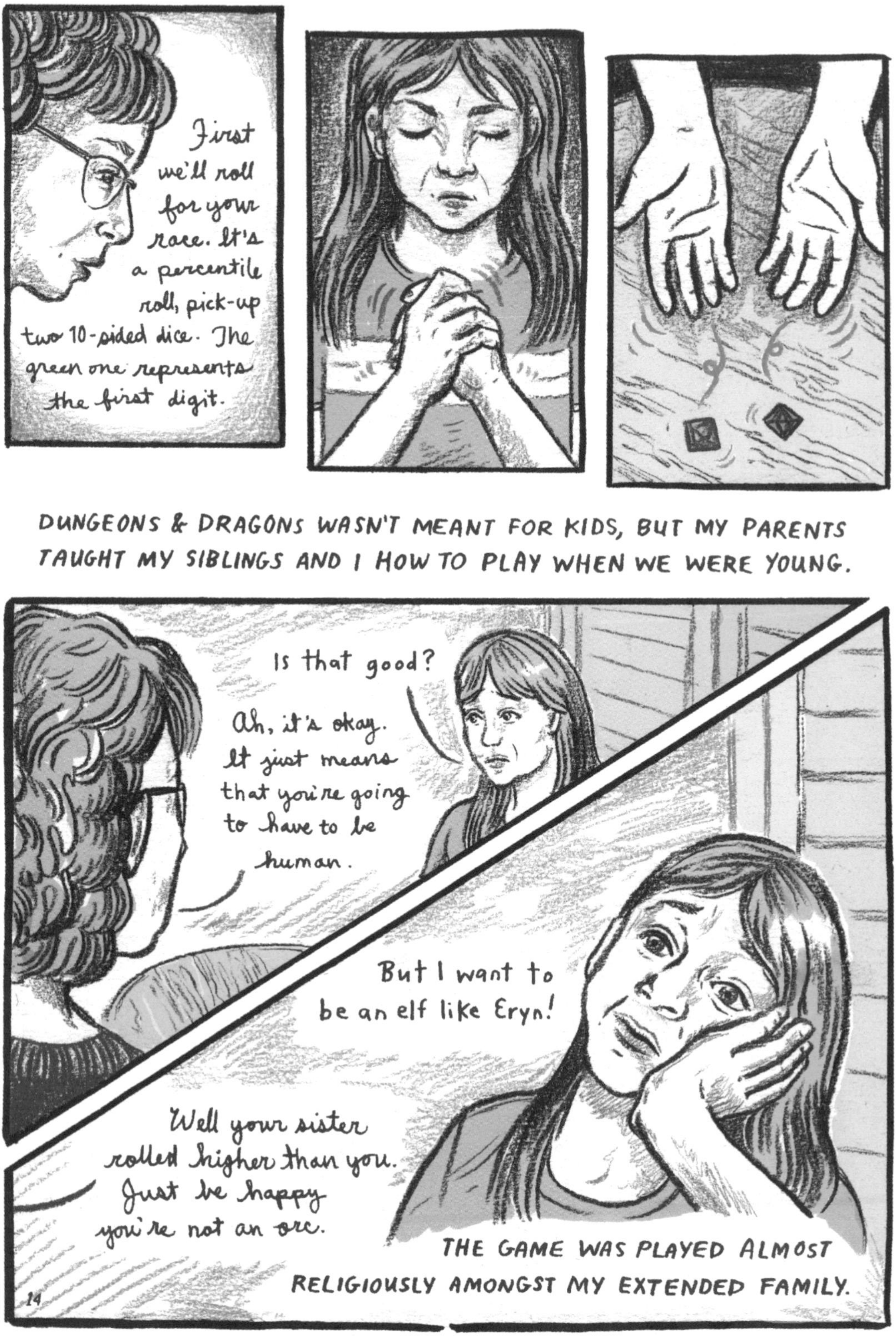
First we'll roll for your race. It's a percentile roll, pick-up two 10-sided dice. The green one represents the first digit.
DUNGEONS & DRAGONS WASN'T MEANT FOR KIDS, BUT MY PARENTS TAUGHT MY SIBLINGS AND I HOW TO PLAY WHEN WE WERE YOUNG.
Is that good?
Ah, it's okay. It just means that you're going to have to be human.
But I want to be an elf like Eryn!
Well your sister rolled higher than you. Just be happy you're not an orc.
THE GAME WAS PLAYED ALMOST RELIGIOUSLY AMONGST MY EXTENDED FAMILY.

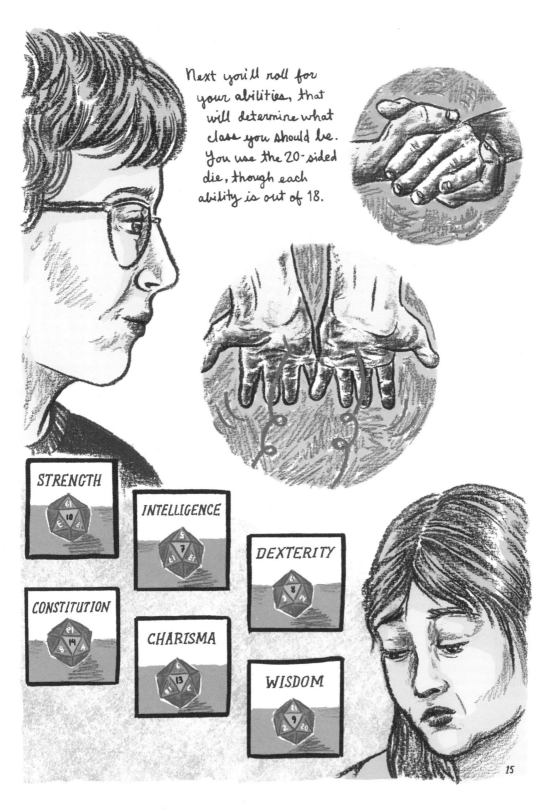

Next you'll roll for your abilities, that will determine what class you should be. You use the 20-sided die, though each ability is out of 18.

STRENGTH

INTELLIGENCE

DEXTERITY

CONSTITUTION

CHARISMA

WISDOM

THEY TAUGHT US SO THAT WE COULD JOIN THEIR WEEKEND-LONG ADVENTURES. WE SLOWED DOWN THE GAME BUT IT WAS EASIER THAN ARRANGING CHILD CARE.

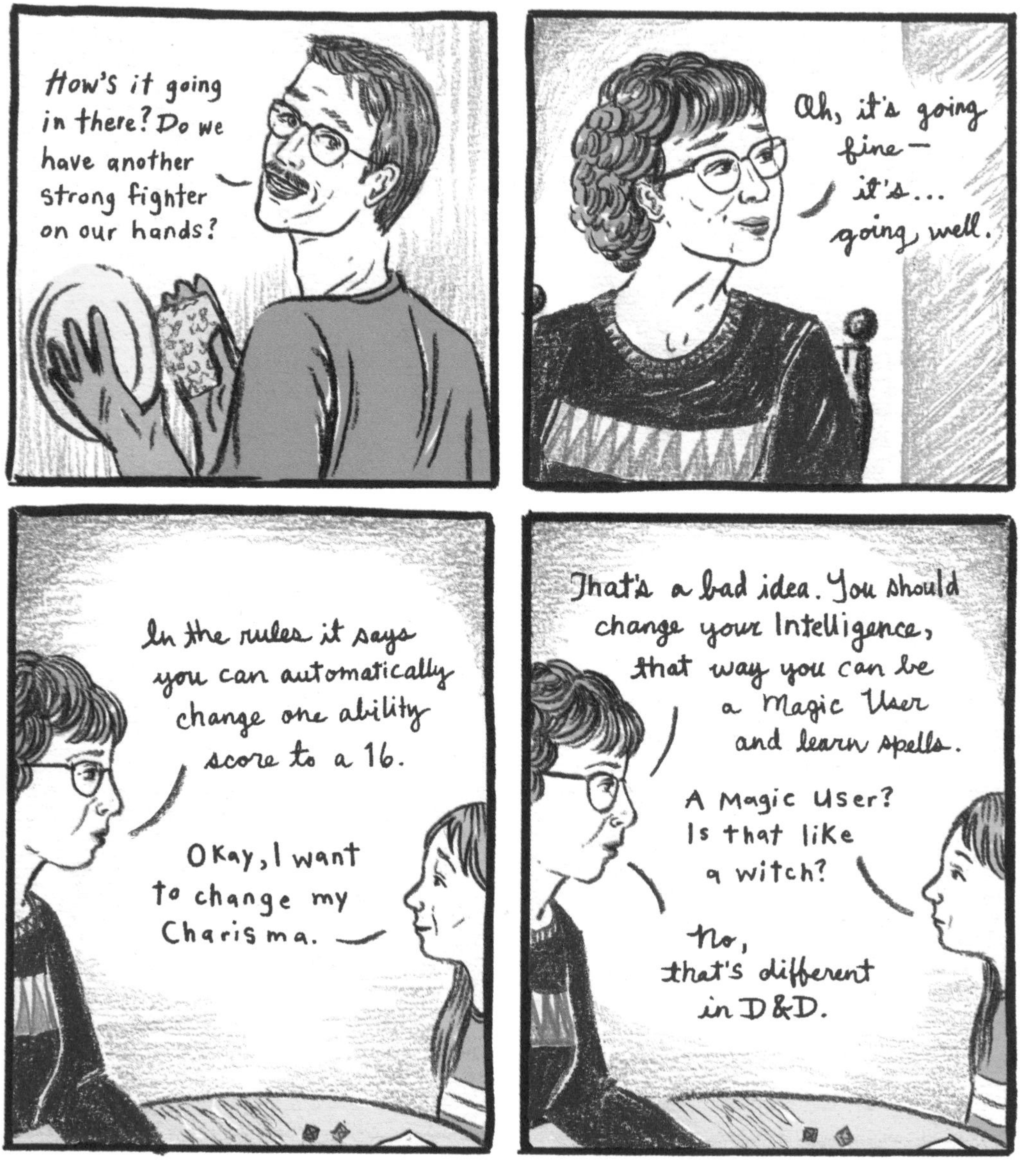

How's it going in there? Do we have another strong fighter on our hands?
Oh, it's going fine — it's... going well.
In the rules it says you can automatically change one ability score to a 16.
Okay, I want to change my Charisma.
That's a bad idea. You should change your Intelligence, that way you can be a Magic User and learn spells.
A Magic User? Is that like a witch?
No, that's different in D&D.

I REALLY LIKED IT. D&D WAS JUST A LONG GAME OF "MAKE BELIEVE" WITH THE ADULTS.

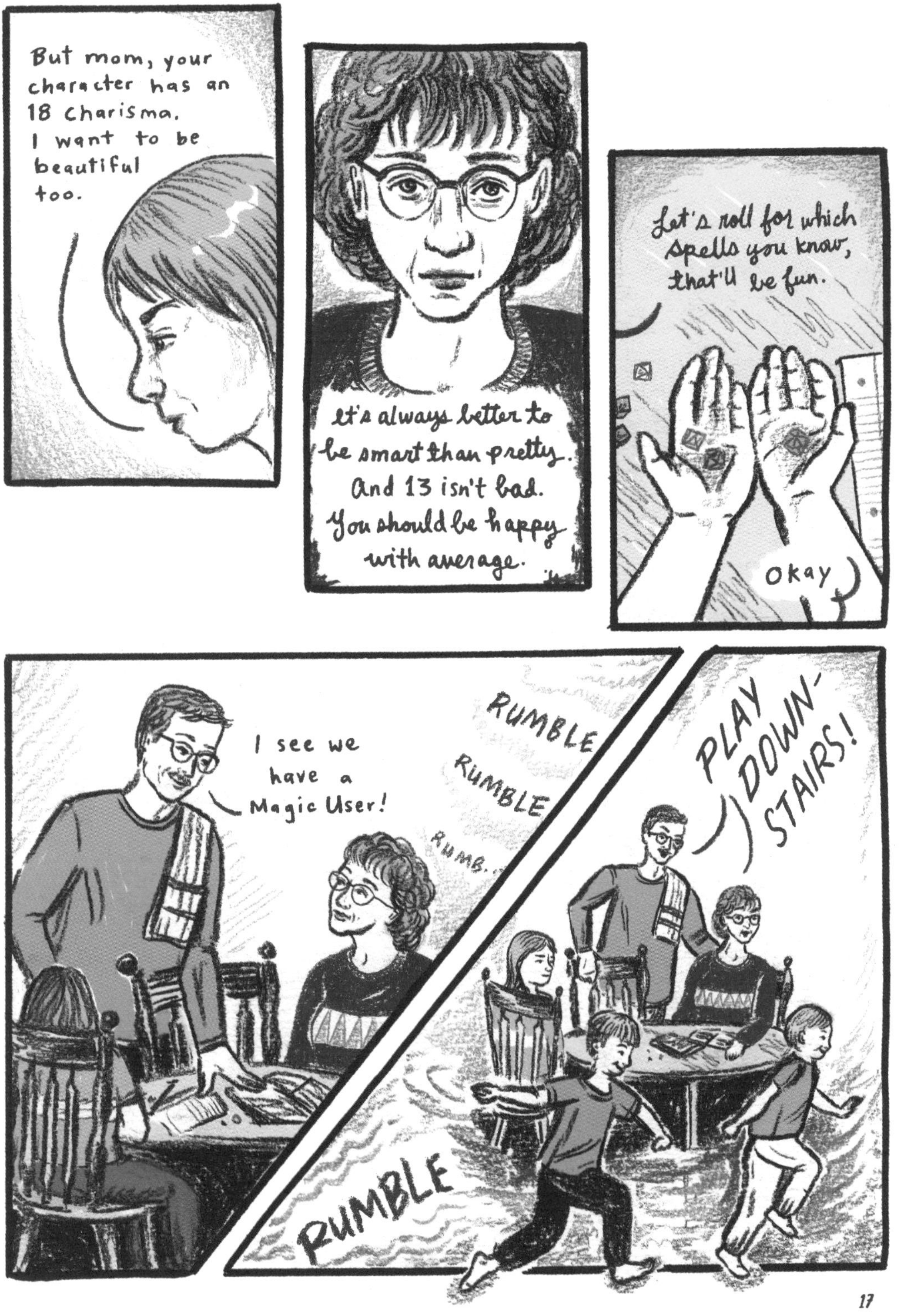
But mom, your character has an 18 Charisma. I want to be beautiful too.
It's always better to be smart than pretty. And 13 isn't bad. You should be happy with average.
Let's roll for which spells you know, that'll be fun.
Okay
I see we have a Magic User!
RUMBLE
RUMBLE
RUMB...
PLAY DOWN-STAIRS!
RUMBLE

But mom there's nothing really special about her. Can she have red hair or do I have to roll for that too?

No, you can pick that. She'll get more special things as she gains experience.

After you're finished that drawing, please do your homework. I've got to put your brothers to bed.

Okay.

Amber the Magic User

'95 '96

In my family I was sandwiched between siblings and at school, bookended by the loud and quiet, the rich and poor, the cool and uncool.

I felt unnoticed and daydreamed, even prayed, for an Ugly Duckling type outcome.

I simultaneously strived to stand out and nestled myself in averageness, a comfortable place for an introvert.

The middle was, if nothing else, safe.

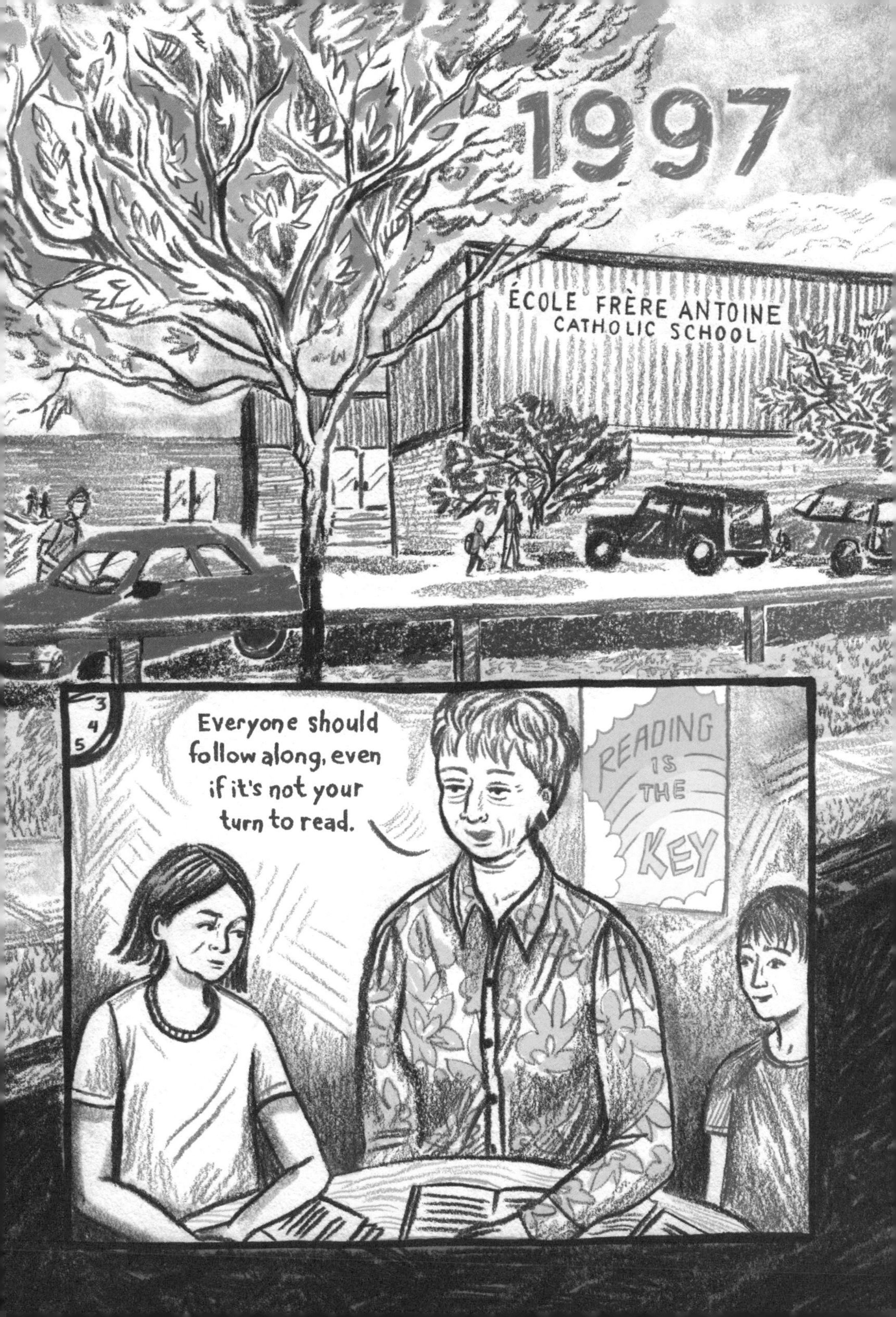
1997
ÉCOLE FRÈRE ANTOINE
CATHOLIC SCHOOL
Everyone should follow along, even if it's not your turn to read.
READING IS THE KEY

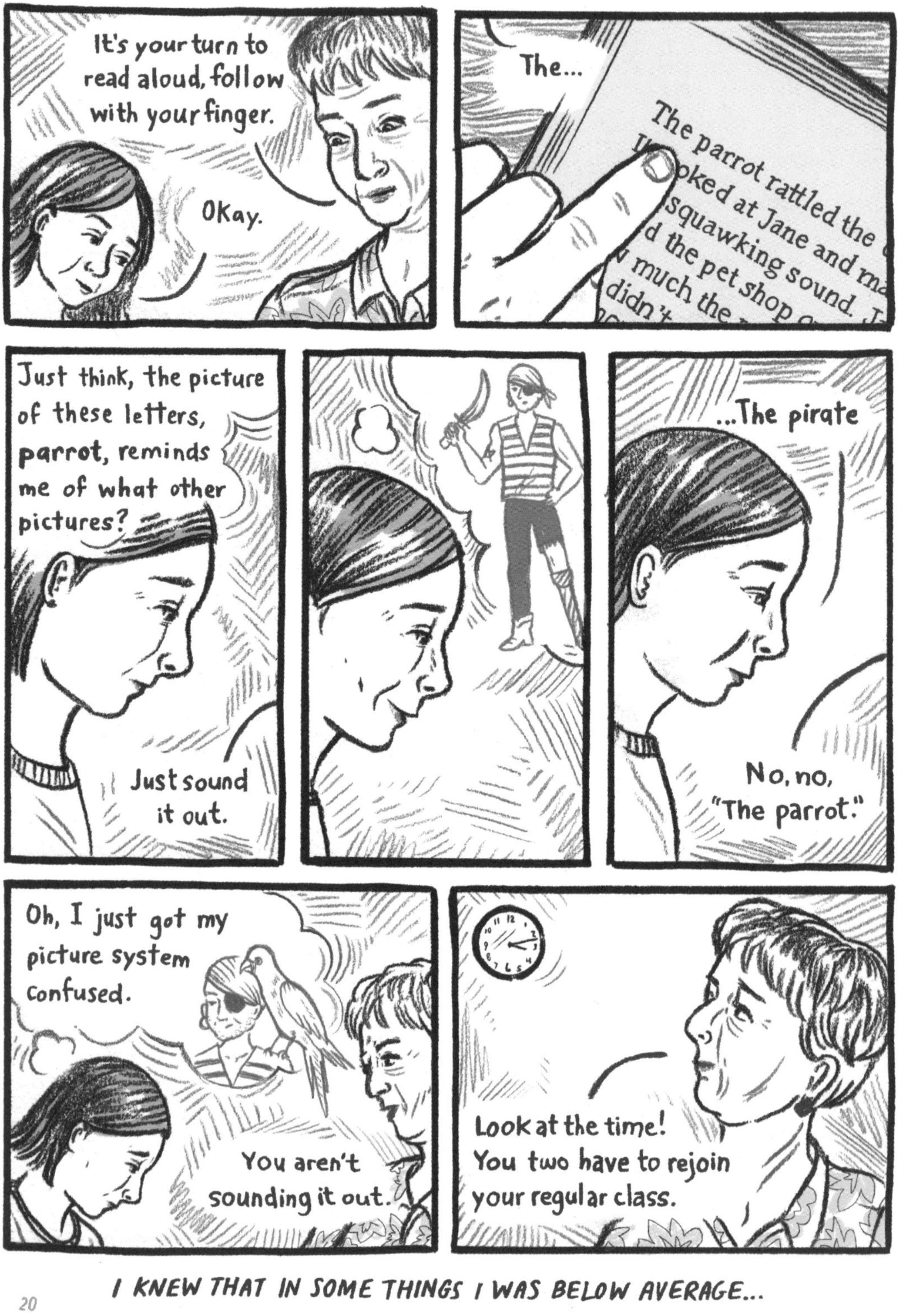
It's your turn to read aloud, follow with your finger.
Okay.
The...
The parrot rattled the
looked at Jane and
squawking sound.
the pet shop
much the
Just think, the picture of these letters, parrot, reminds me of what other pictures?
Just sound it out.
...The pirate
No, no, "The parrot."
Oh, I just got my picture system confused.
You aren't sounding it out.
Look at the time! You two have to rejoin your regular class.

I KNEW THAT IN SOME THINGS I WAS BELOW AVERAGE...

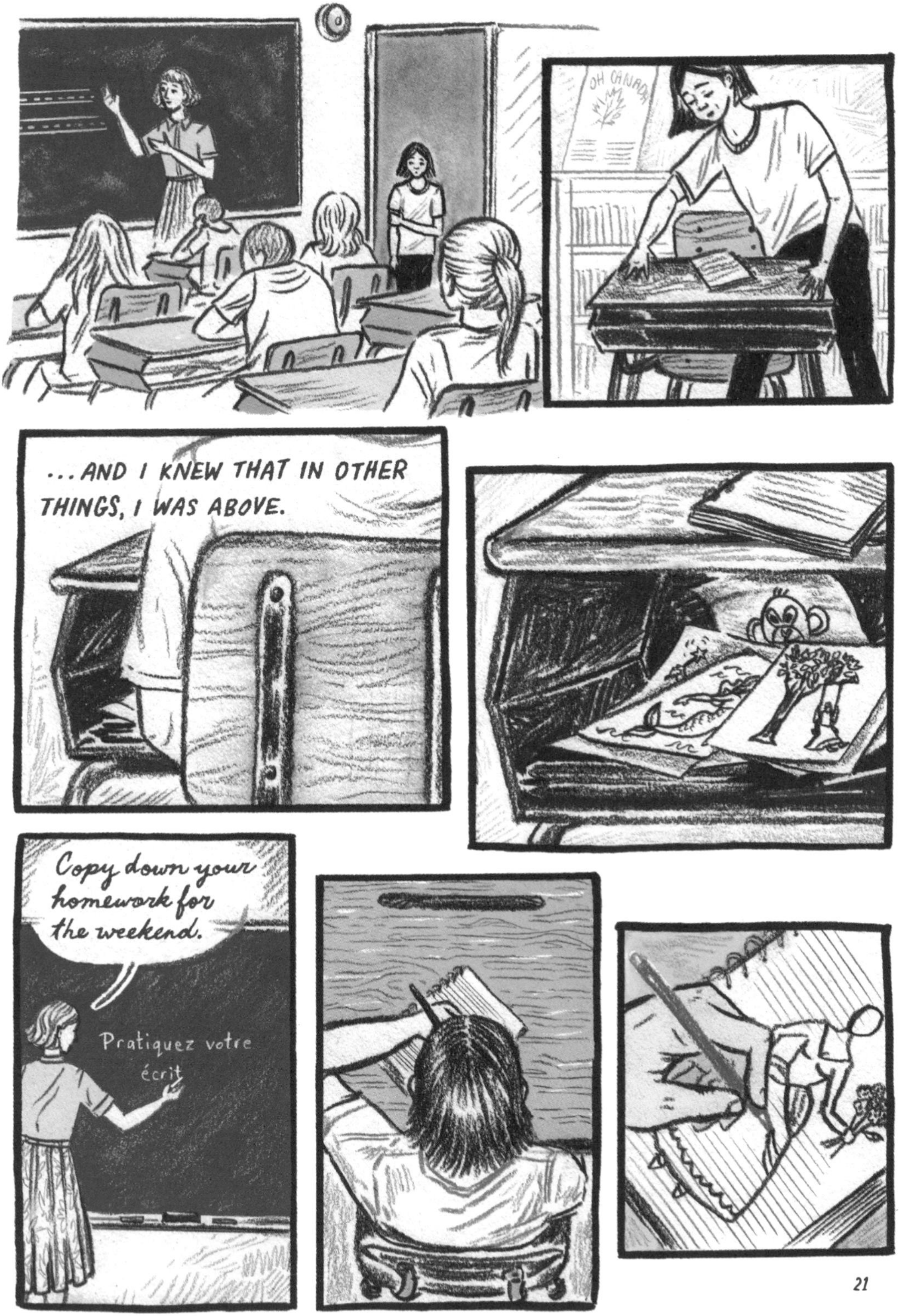
OH CANADA
...AND I KNEW THAT IN OTHER THINGS, I WAS ABOVE.
Copy down your homework for the weekend.
Pratiquez votre écrit

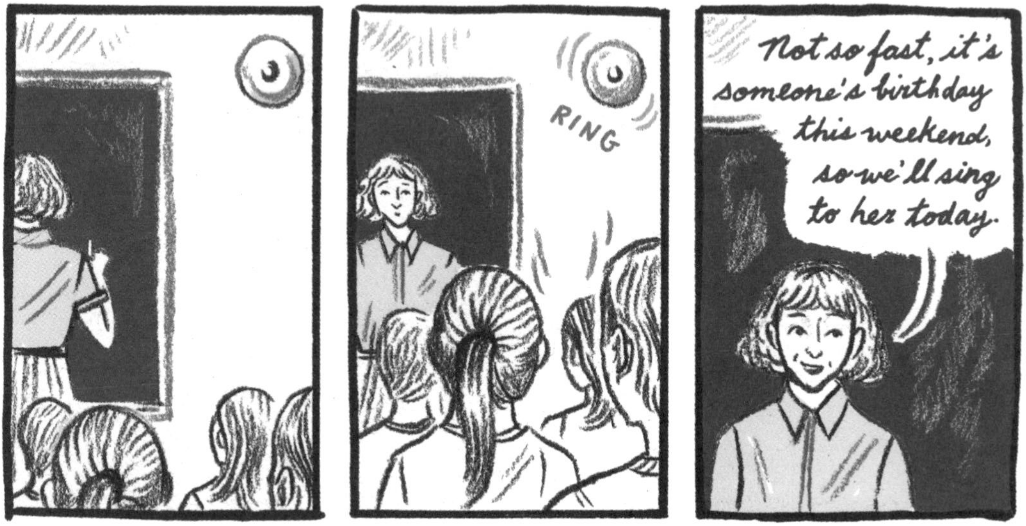
RING
Not so fast, it's someone's birthday this weekend, so we'll sing to her today.

MY NATURAL COMPLEXION IS GHOST-WHITE, WITH CHEEKS THAT BLUSH EASILY AND BROWN HAIR THAT SHINES AUBURN IN THE SUN.

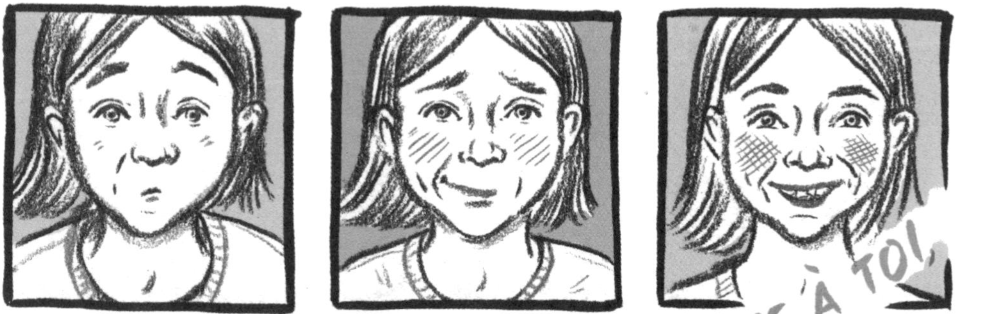

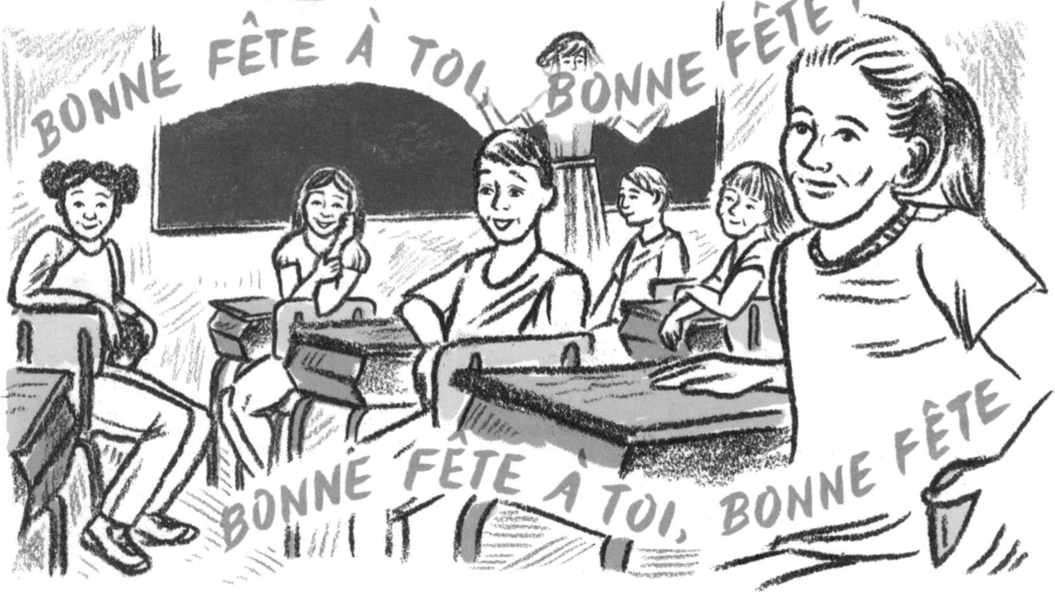
BONNE FÊTE À TOI, BONNE FÊTE À TOI,
BONNE FÊTE À TOI, BONNE FÊTE

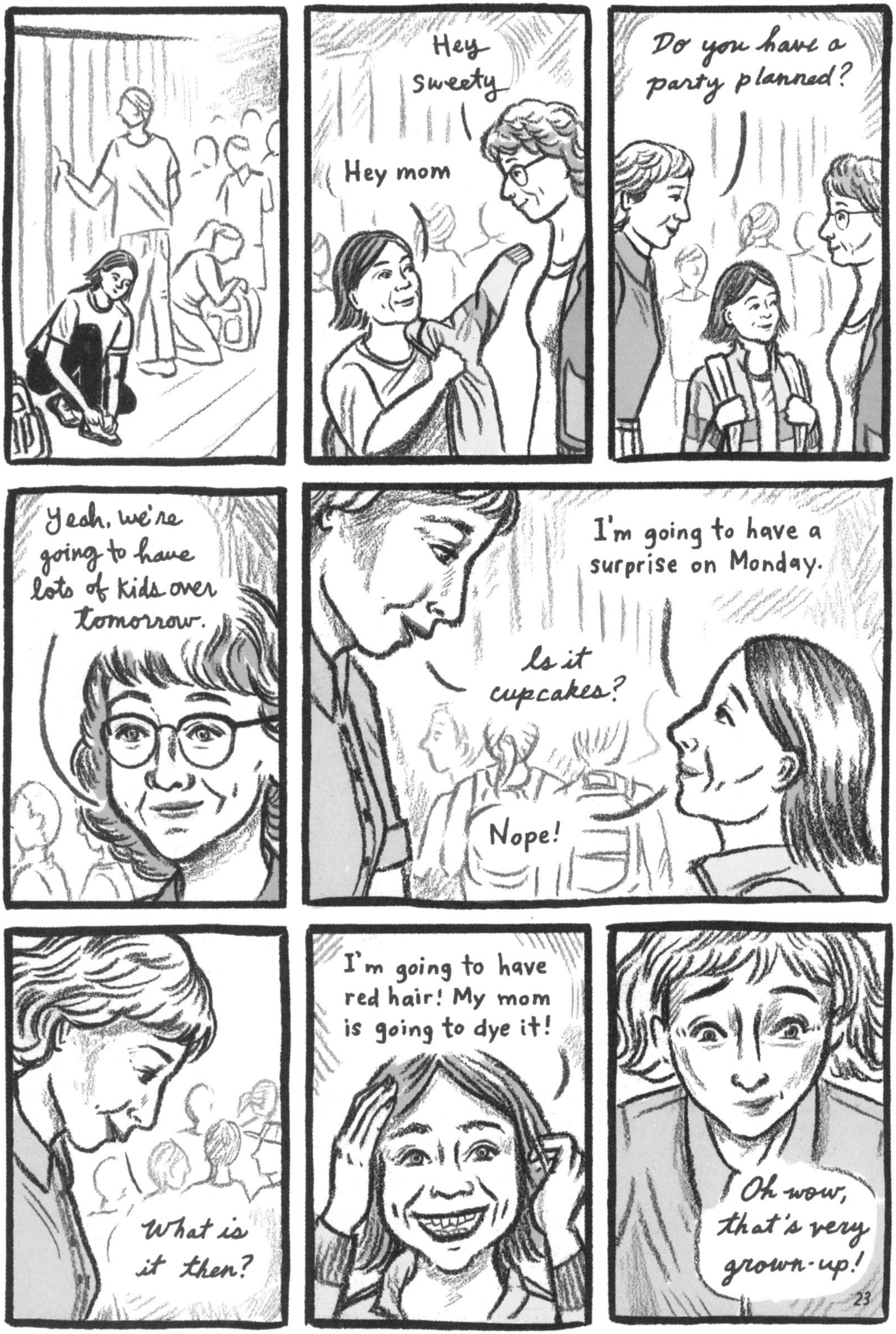
Hey sweety
Hey mom
Do you have a party planned?
Yeah, we're going to have lots of kids over tomorrow.
I'm going to have a surprise on Monday.
Is it cupcakes?
Nope!
What is it then?
I'm going to have red hair! My mom is going to dye it!
Oh wow, that's very grown-up!

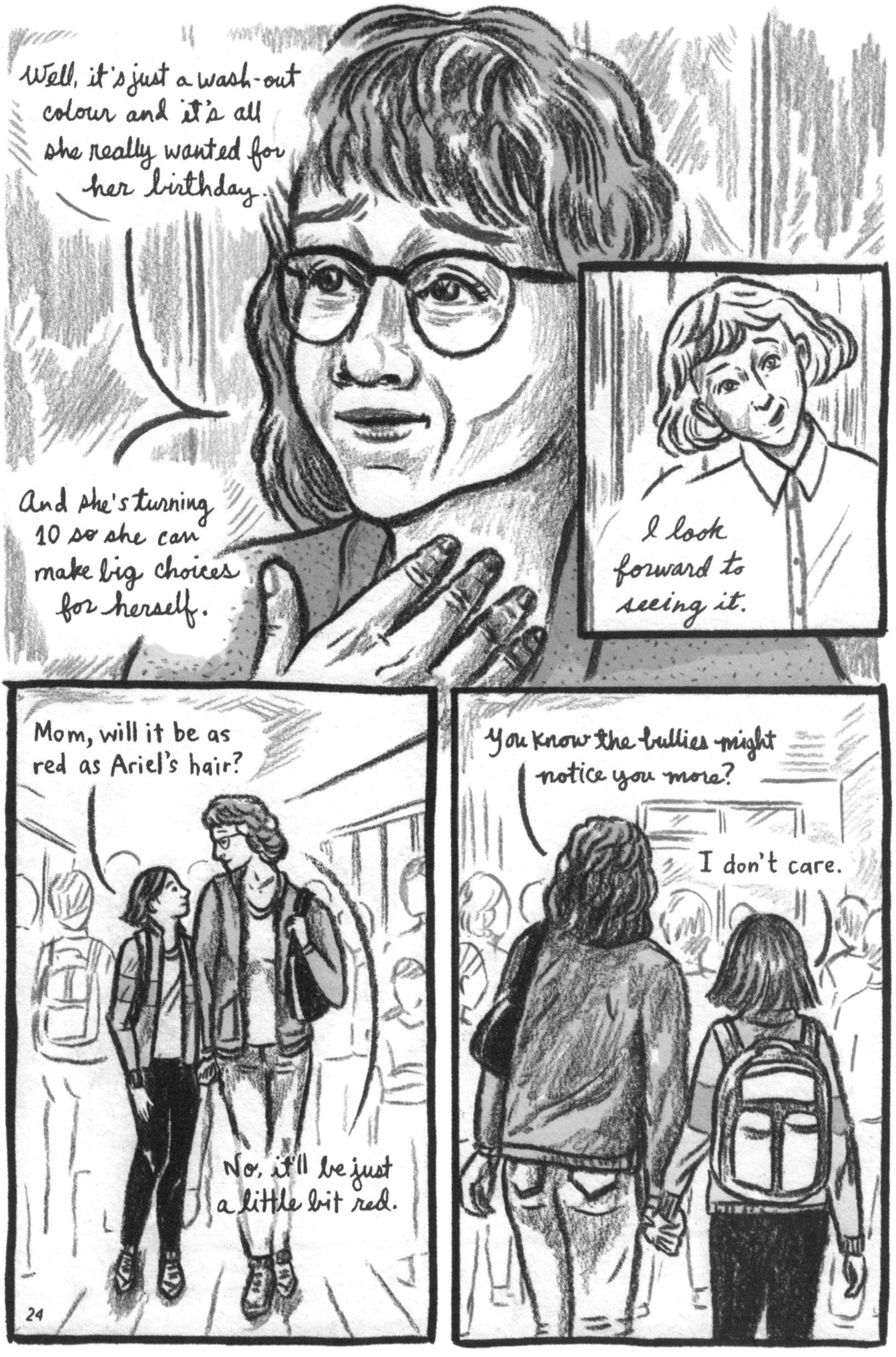
Well, it's just a wash-out colour and it's all she really wanted for her birthday.
And she's turning 10 so she can make big choices for herself.
I look forward to seeing it.
Mom, will it be as red as Ariel's hair?
No, it'll be just a little bit red.
You know the bullies might notice you more?
I don't care.

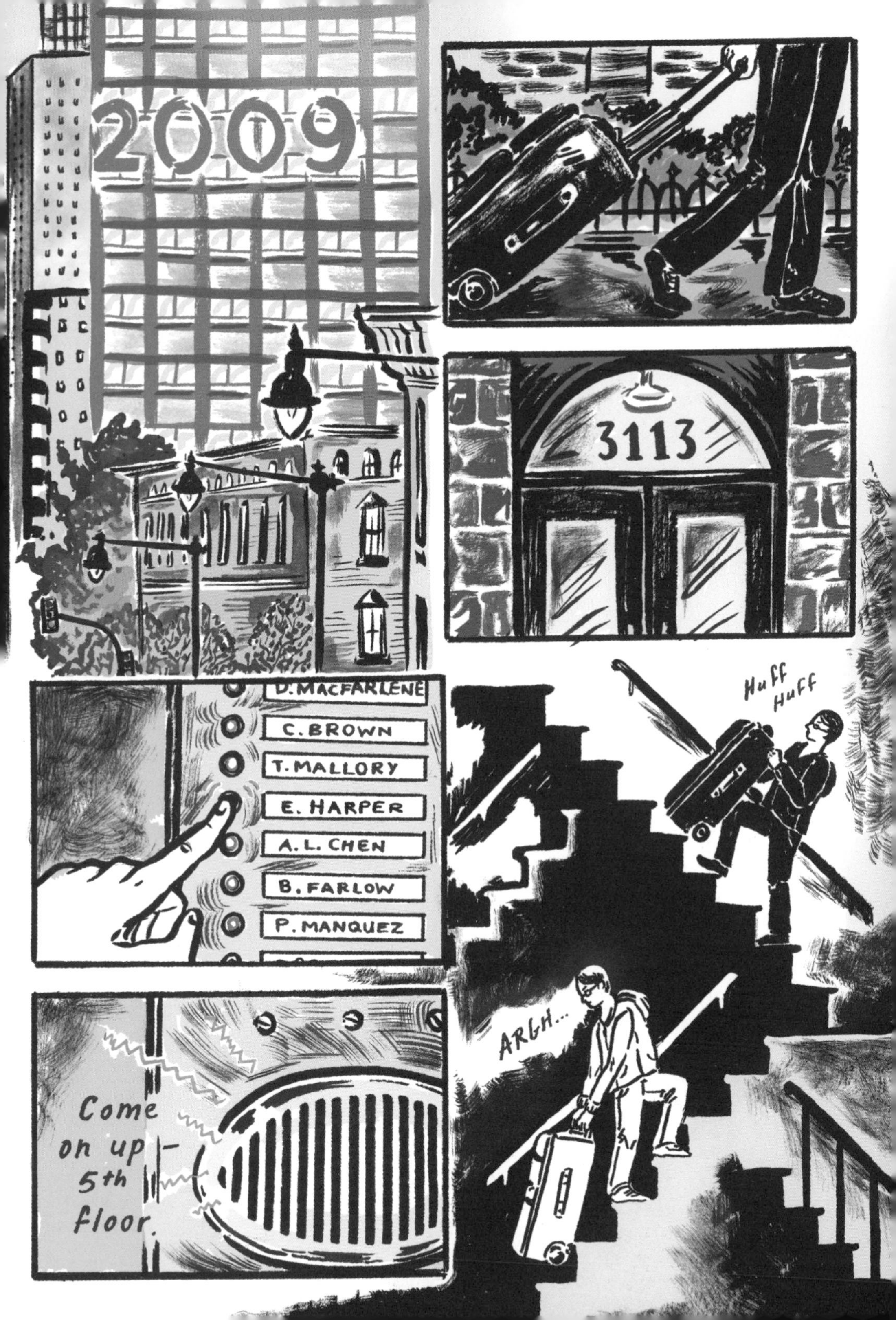
2009
3113
D. MACFARLENE
C. BROWN
T. MALLORY
E. HARPER
A. L. CHEN
B. FARLOW
P. MANQUEZ
Huff Huff
Come on up — 5th floor.
ARGH...

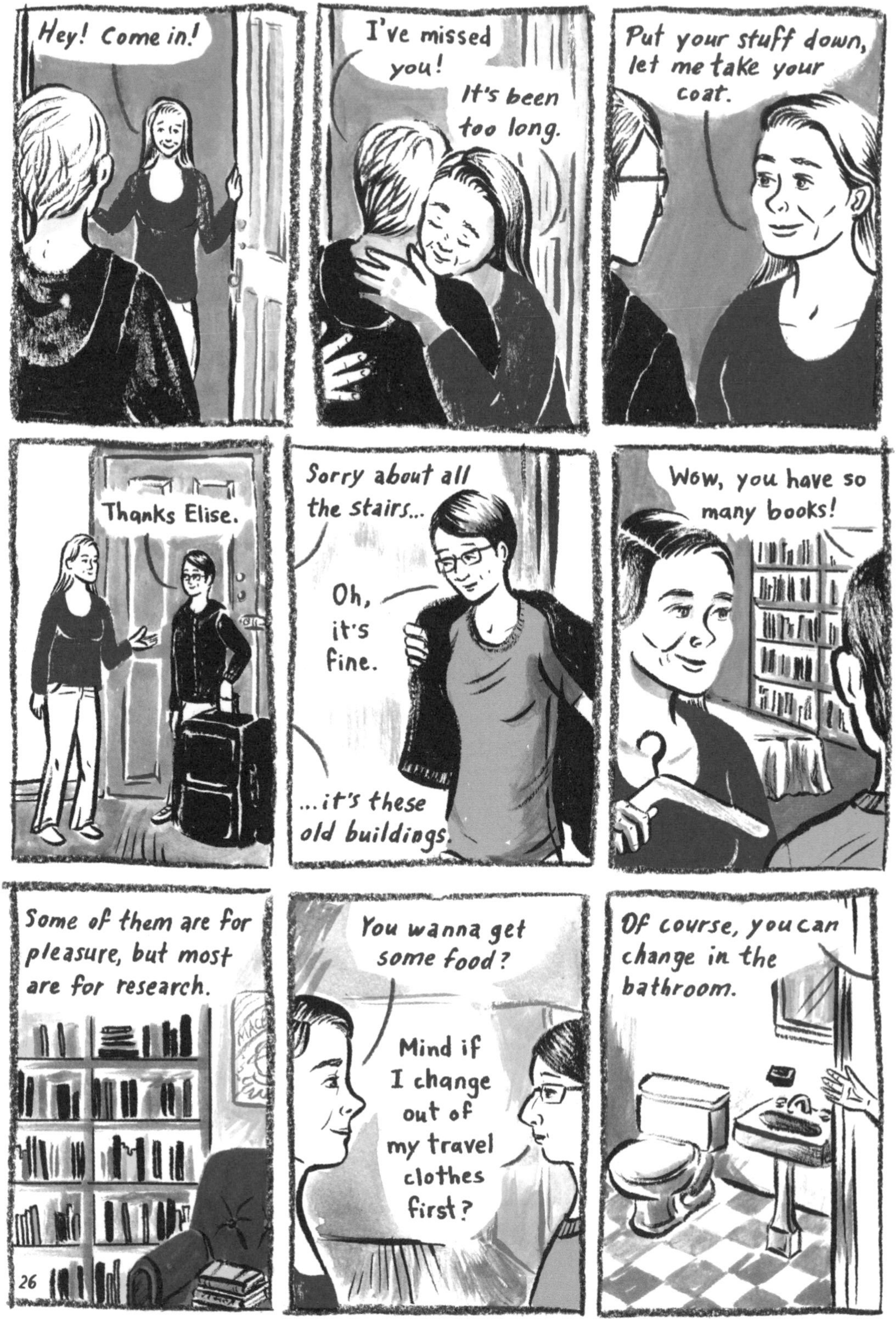
Hey! Come in!
I've missed you!
It's been too long.
Put your stuff down, let me take your coat.
Thanks Elise.
Sorry about all the stairs...
Oh, it's fine.
...it's these old buildings.
Wow, you have so many books!
Some of them are for pleasure, but most are for research.
You wanna get some food?
Mind if I change out of my travel clothes first?
Of course, you can change in the bathroom.

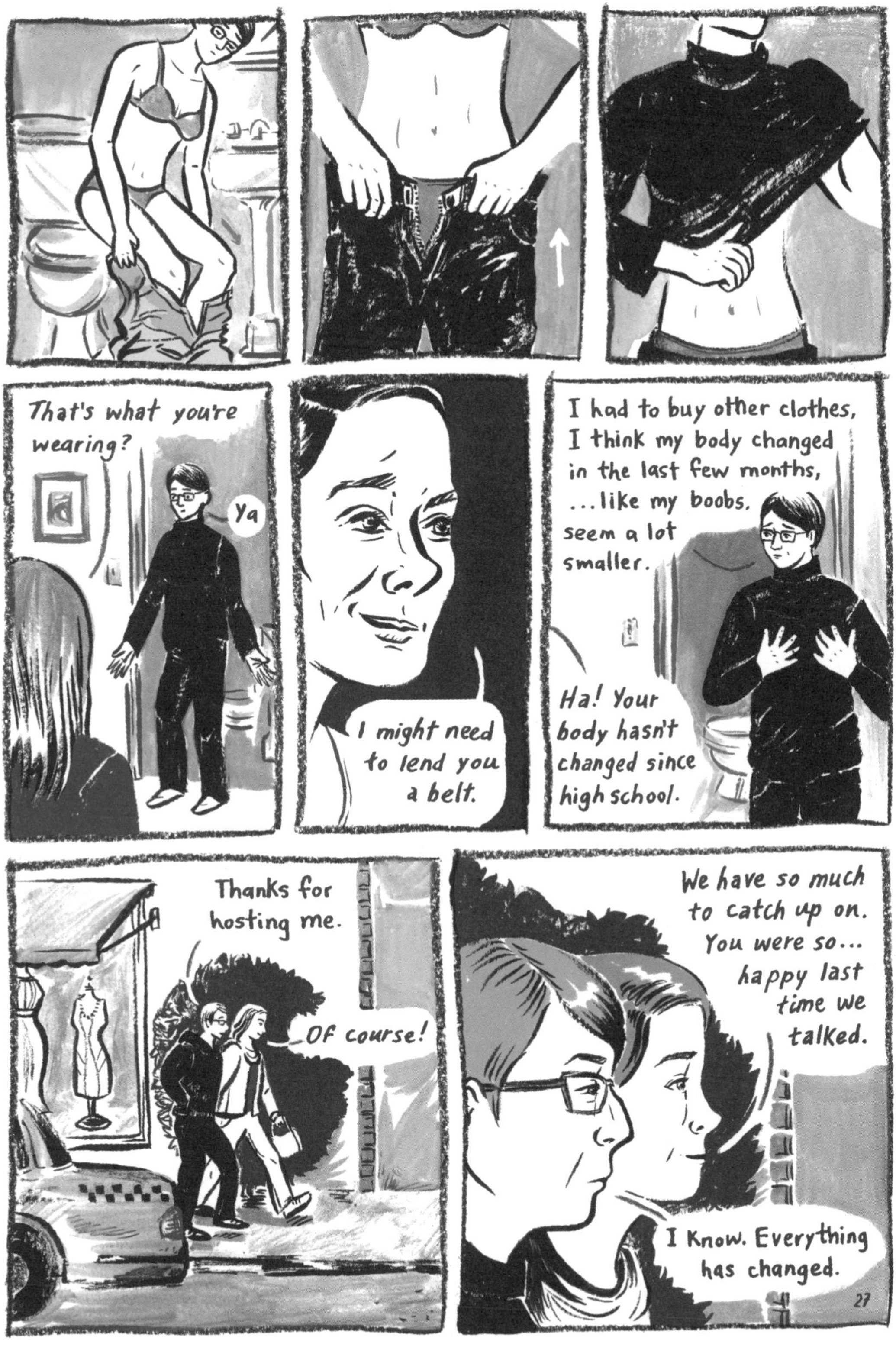

That's what you're wearing?
Ya
I might need to lend you a belt.
I had to buy other clothes, I think my body changed in the last few months, ...like my boobs, seem a lot smaller.
Ha! Your body hasn't changed since high school.
Thanks for hosting me.
Of course!
We have so much to catch up on. You were so... happy last time we talked.
I Know. Everything has changed.

IN COLLEGE I HAD A HAIR-STYLIST THAT I DID HAIR-MODELING FOR. SHE'D GIVE ME AWESOME HAIRCUTS FOR FREE, BUT I DIDN'T GET TO CHOOSE THE STYLE. THE PIXIE CUT WAS HER IDEA BUT I LIKED IT.

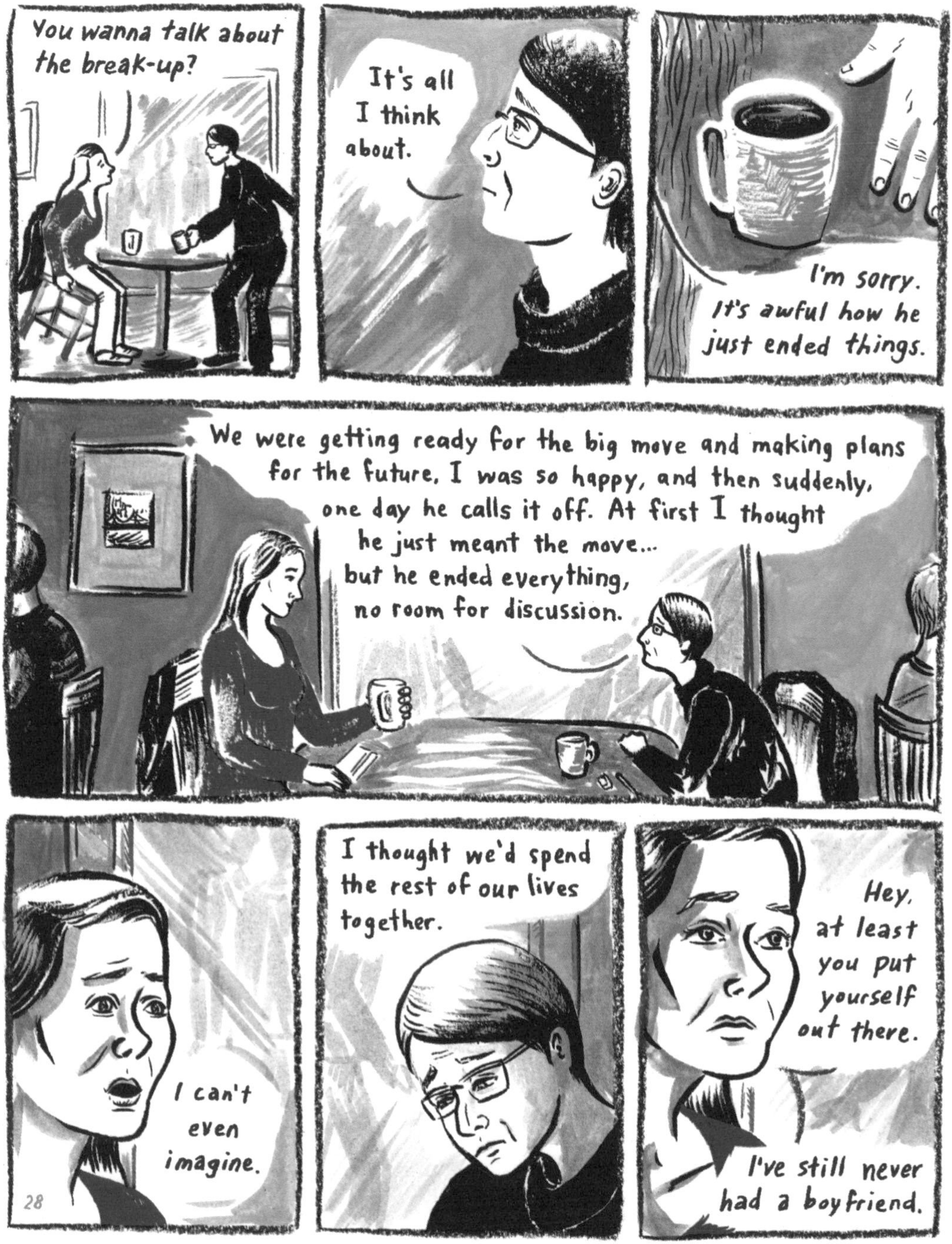

You wanna talk about the break-up?
It's all I think about.
I'm sorry. It's awful how he just ended things.
We were getting ready for the big move and making plans for the future. I was so happy, and then suddenly, one day he calls it off. At first I thought he just meant the move... but he ended everything, no room for discussion.
I can't even imagine.
I thought we'd spend the rest of our lives together.
Hey, at least you put yourself out there.
I've still never had a boyfriend.

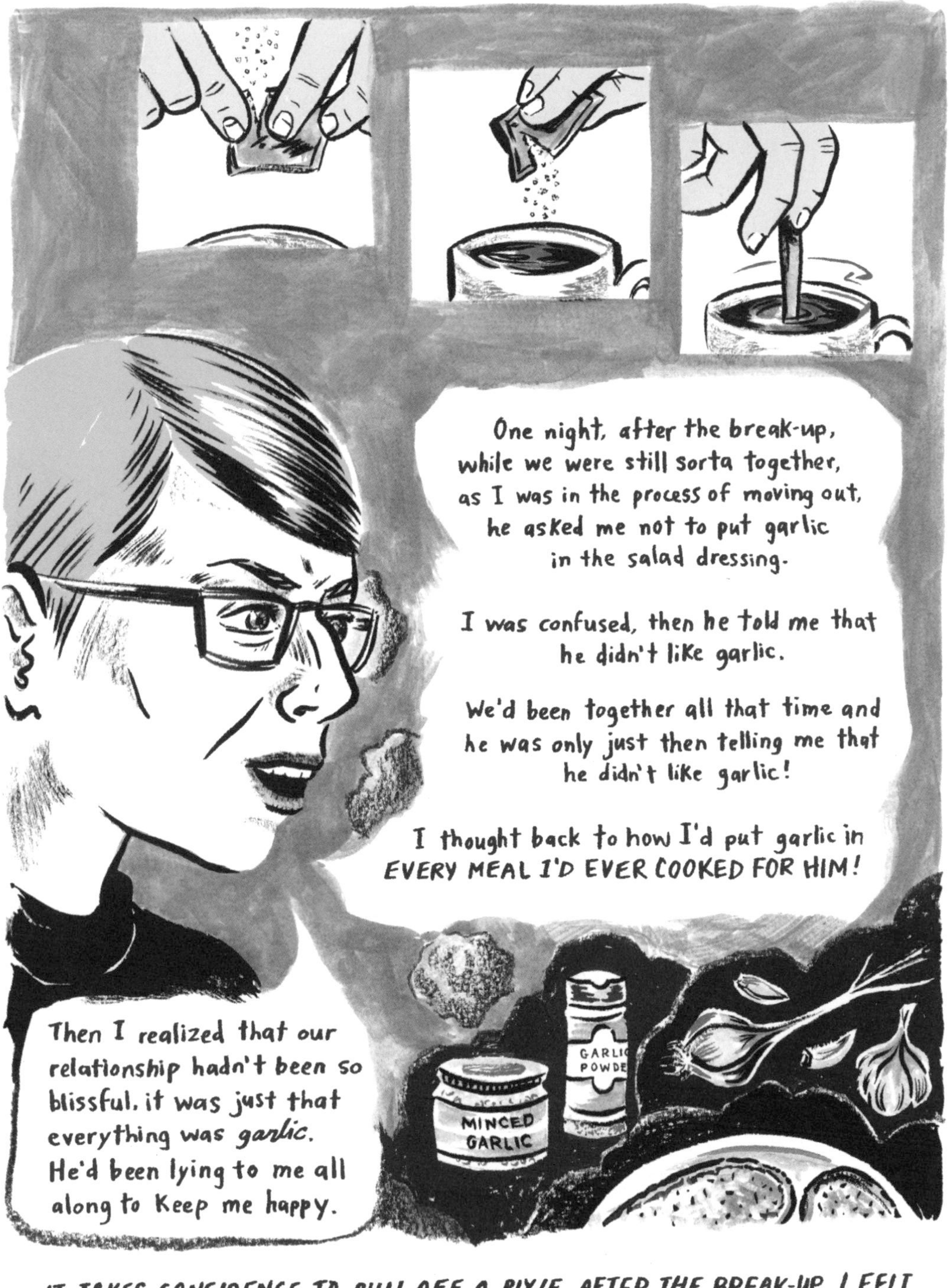
One night, after the break-up, while we were still sorta together, as I was in the process of moving out, he asked me not to put garlic in the salad dressing.
I was confused, then he told me that he didn't like garlic.
We'd been together all that time and he was only just then telling me that he didn't like garlic!
I thought back to how I'd put garlic in EVERY MEAL I'D EVER COOKED FOR HIM!
Then I realized that our relationship hadn't been so blissful. it was just that everything was *garlic*. He'd been lying to me all along to keep me happy.
MINCED GARLIC

IT TAKES CONFIDENCE TO PULL OFF A PIXIE. AFTER THE BREAK-UP, I FELT EXPOSED AND UNFEMININE. ALL I WANTED WAS FOR MY HAIR TO GROW BACK.

When everything falls apart, it takes some time to rebuild.

It's only been a few months, you'll feel like your old self again soon.

I don't think I'll ever be able to trust anyone ever again.

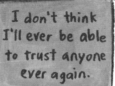

You feel that way now, but in a few months I bet you'll be dating again.

I can't even fathom that. When I see someone attractive, I just avoid eye contact, they're just too intimidating.

I wouldn't risk embarrassing myself by assuming anyone would ever be into me.

Sorry, we can change the subject, I haven't stopped talking about myself since I arrived.

What are you writing these days?

I'm working on a new play.

I just picked this up at a used bookstore for research.

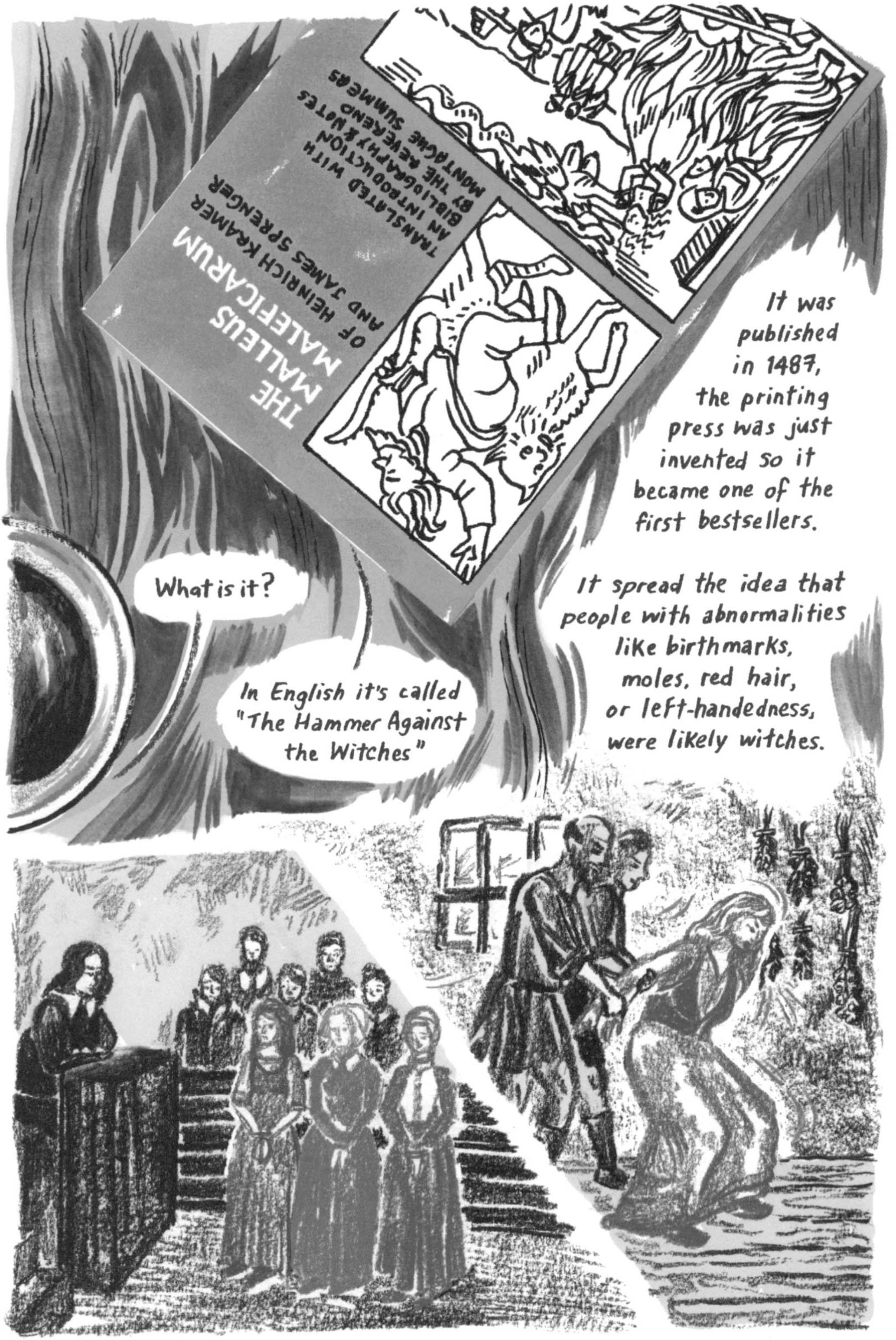
THE MALLEUS MALEFICARUM
OF HEINRICH KRAMER AND JAMES SPRENGER
TRANSLATED WITH AN INTRODUCTION BIBLIOGRAPHY & NOTES BY THE REVEREND MONTAGUE SUMMERS
It was published in 1487, the printing press was just invented so it became one of the first bestsellers.
What is it?
In English it's called "The Hammer Against the Witches"
It spread the idea that people with abnormalities like birthmarks, moles, red hair, or left-handedness, were likely witches.

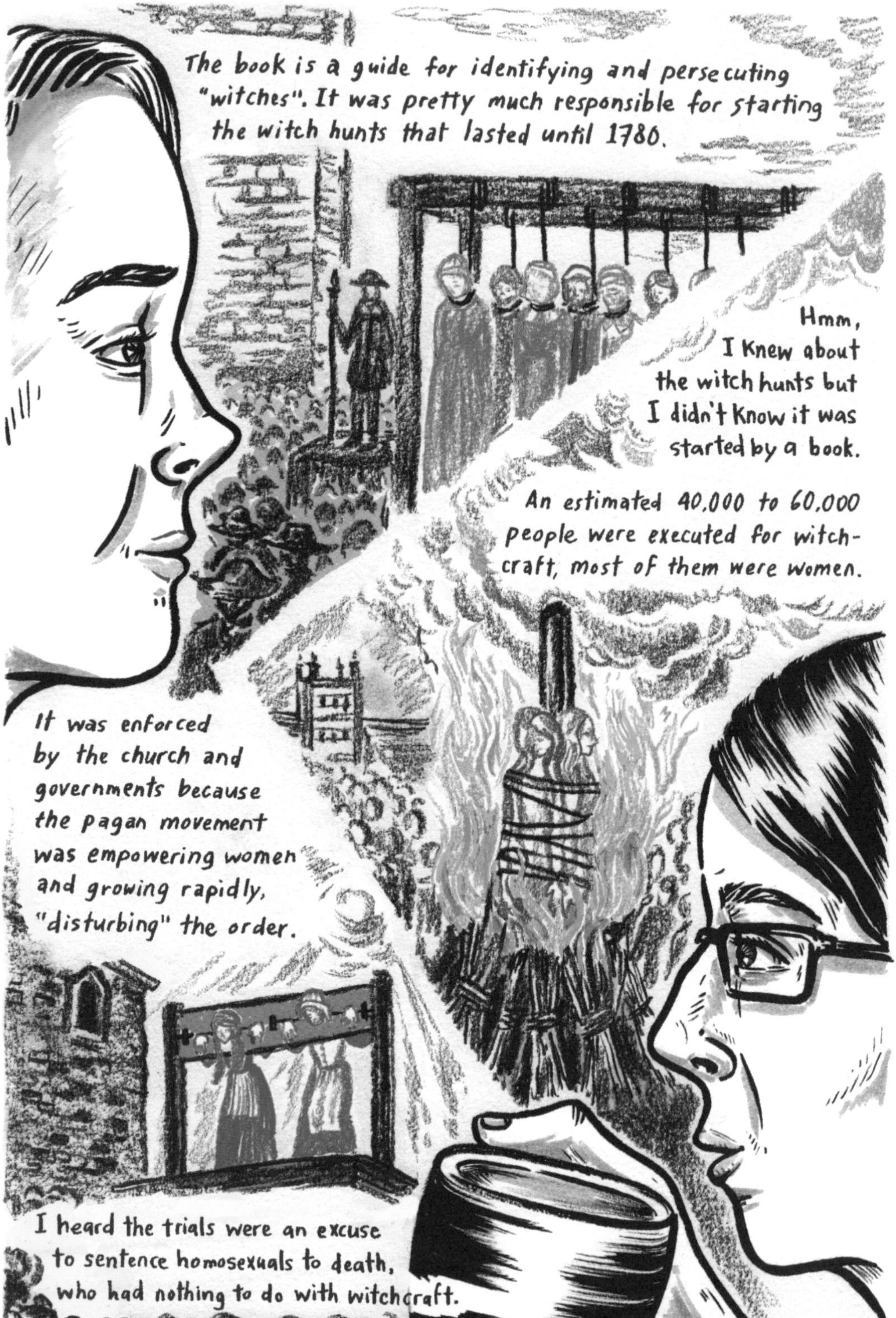
The book is a guide for identifying and persecuting "witches". It was pretty much responsible for starting the witch hunts that lasted until 1780.
Hmm, I knew about the witch hunts but I didn't know it was started by a book.
An estimated 40,000 to 60,000 people were executed for witchcraft, most of them were women.
It was enforced by the church and governments because the pagan movement was empowering women and growing rapidly, "disturbing" the order.
I heard the trials were an excuse to sentence homosexuals to death, who had nothing to do with witchcraft.

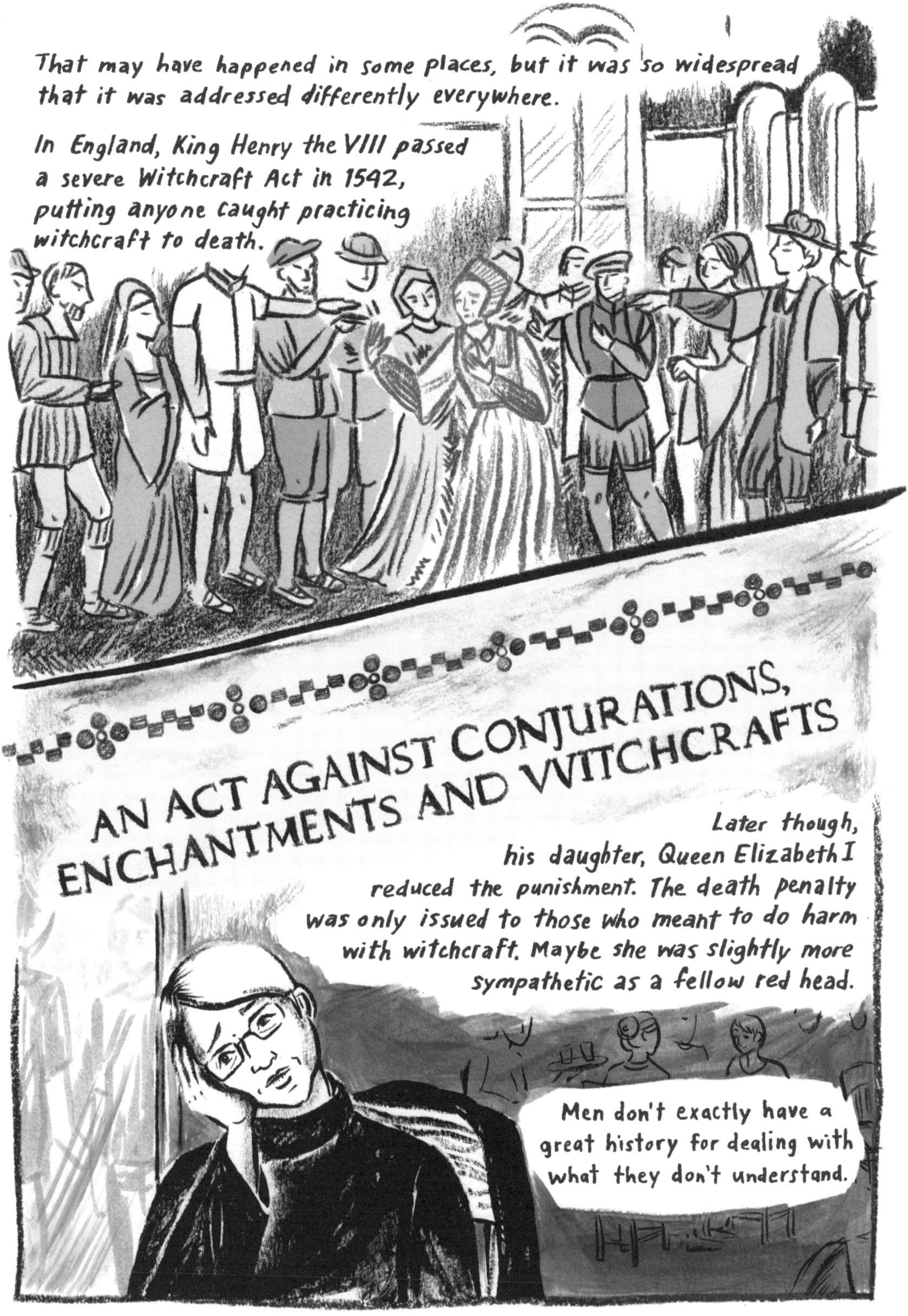
That may have happened in some places, but it was so widespread that it was addressed differently everywhere.
In England, King Henry the VIII passed a severe Witchcraft Act in 1542, putting anyone caught practicing witchcraft to death.
AN ACT AGAINST CONJURATIONS, ENCHANTMENTS AND WITCHCRAFTS
Later though, his daughter, Queen Elizabeth I reduced the punishment. The death penalty was only issued to those who meant to do harm with witchcraft. Maybe she was slightly more sympathetic as a fellow red head.
Men don't exactly have a great history for dealing with what they don't understand.

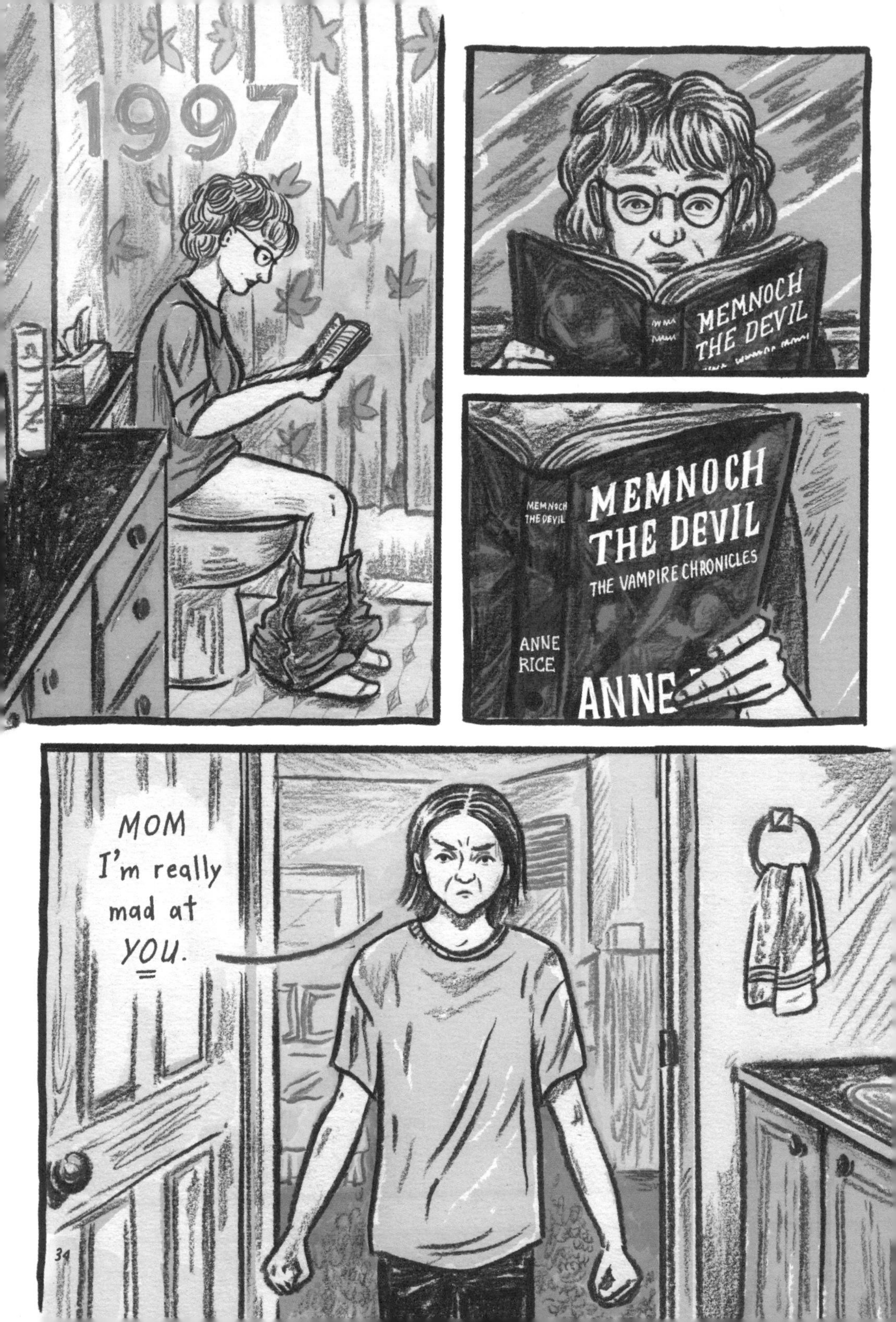
1997
MEMNOCH THE DEVIL
MEMNOCH THE DEVIL
MEMNOCH THE DEVIL
THE VAMPIRE CHRONICLES
ANNE RICE
ANNE
MOM I'm really mad at YOU.

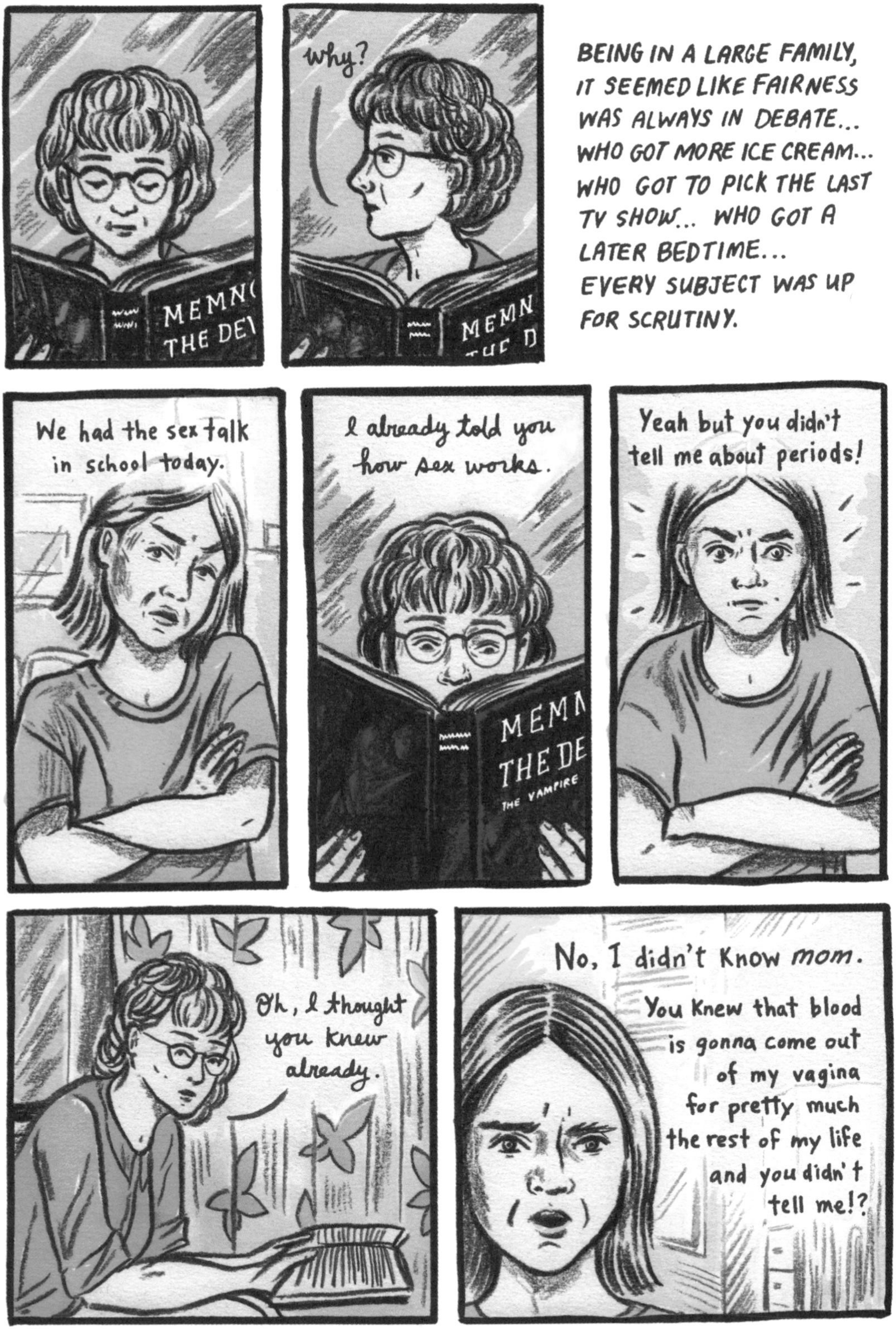
why?
BEING IN A LARGE FAMILY, IT SEEMED LIKE FAIRNESS WAS ALWAYS IN DEBATE... WHO GOT MORE ICE CREAM... WHO GOT TO PICK THE LAST TV SHOW... WHO GOT A LATER BEDTIME... EVERY SUBJECT WAS UP FOR SCRUTINY.
We had the sex talk in school today.
I already told you how sex works.
Yeah but you didn't tell me about periods!
Oh, I thought you knew already.
No, I didn't Know *mom*.
You Knew that blood is gonna come out of my vagina for pretty much the rest of my life and you didn't tell me!?

What did you think the pads & tampons in my purse were for?

I dunno, I just thought something was wrong with you, not with all women!

Nope, sorry. Welcome to being female.

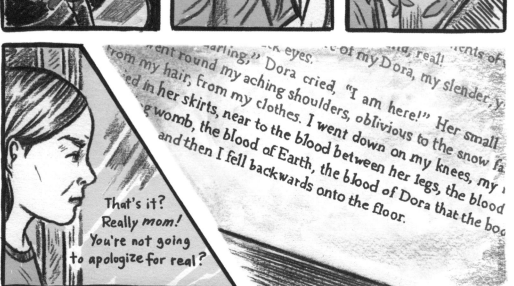

That's it? Really *mom*! You're not going to apologize for real?

...ck eyes. ...e of my Dora, my slender, y... real! ...arling," Dora cried, "I am here!" Her small ...ent round my aching shoulders, oblivious to the snow fa... ...from my hair, from my clothes. I went down on my knees, my ...ed in her skirts, near to the blood between her legs, the blood ...g womb, the blood of Earth, the blood of Dora that the boo... and then I fell backwards onto the floor.

I'm sorry, it's just the way it is.

you have a few years before you'll get it anyway

Does dad know about this?

Of course.

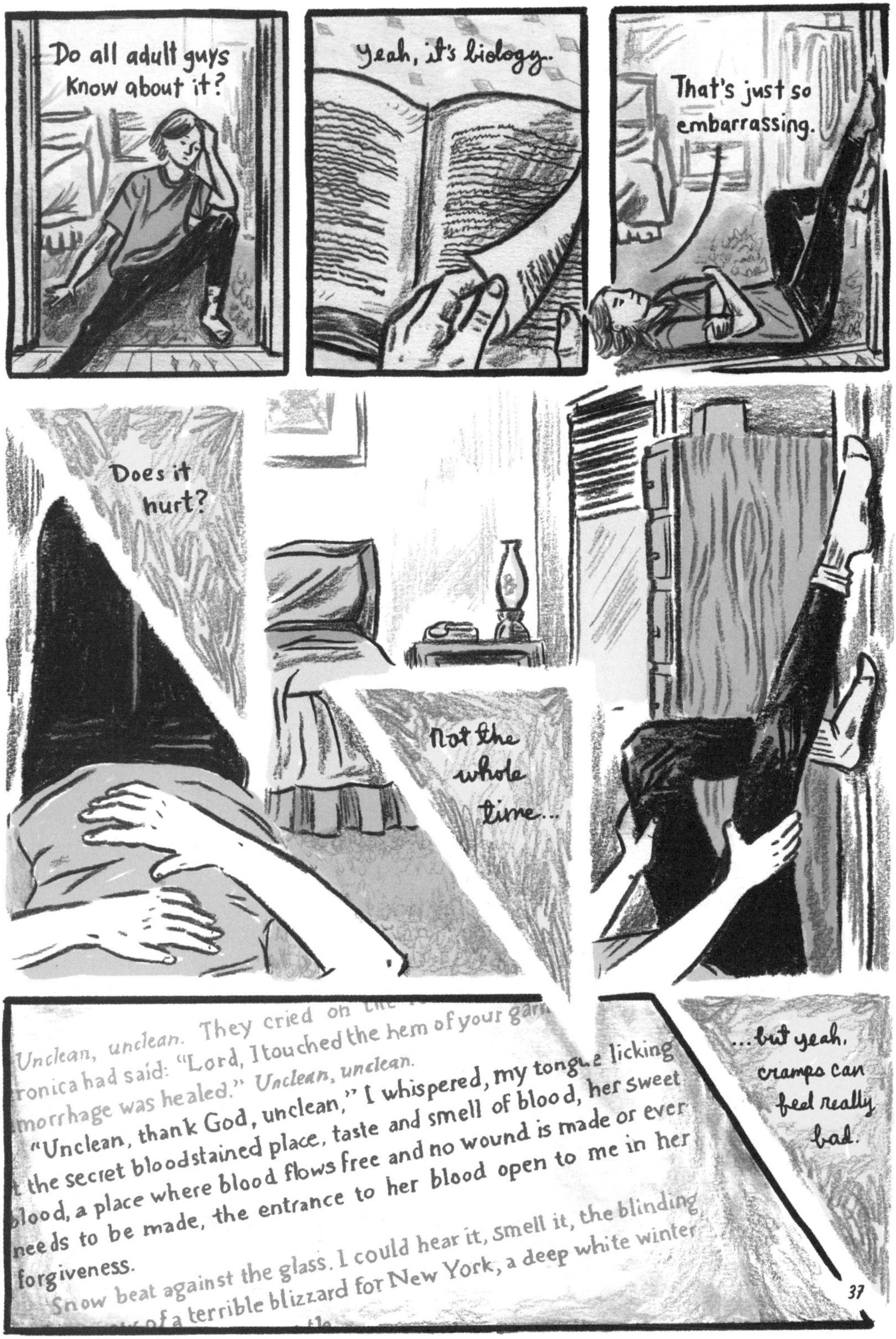
Do all adult guys know about it?
Yeah, it's biology.
That's just so embarrassing.
Does it hurt?
Not the whole time...
Unclean, unclean. They cried on the
ronica had said: "Lord, I touched the hem of your gar
morrhage was healed." Unclean, unclean.
"Unclean, thank God, unclean," I whispered, my tongue licking
t the secret bloodstained place, taste and smell of blood, her sweet
blood, a place where blood flows free and no wound is made or ever
needs to be made, the entrance to her blood open to me in her
forgiveness.
Snow beat against the glass. I could hear it, smell it, the blinding
of a terrible blizzard for New York, a deep white winter
...but yeah, cramps can feel really bad.
37

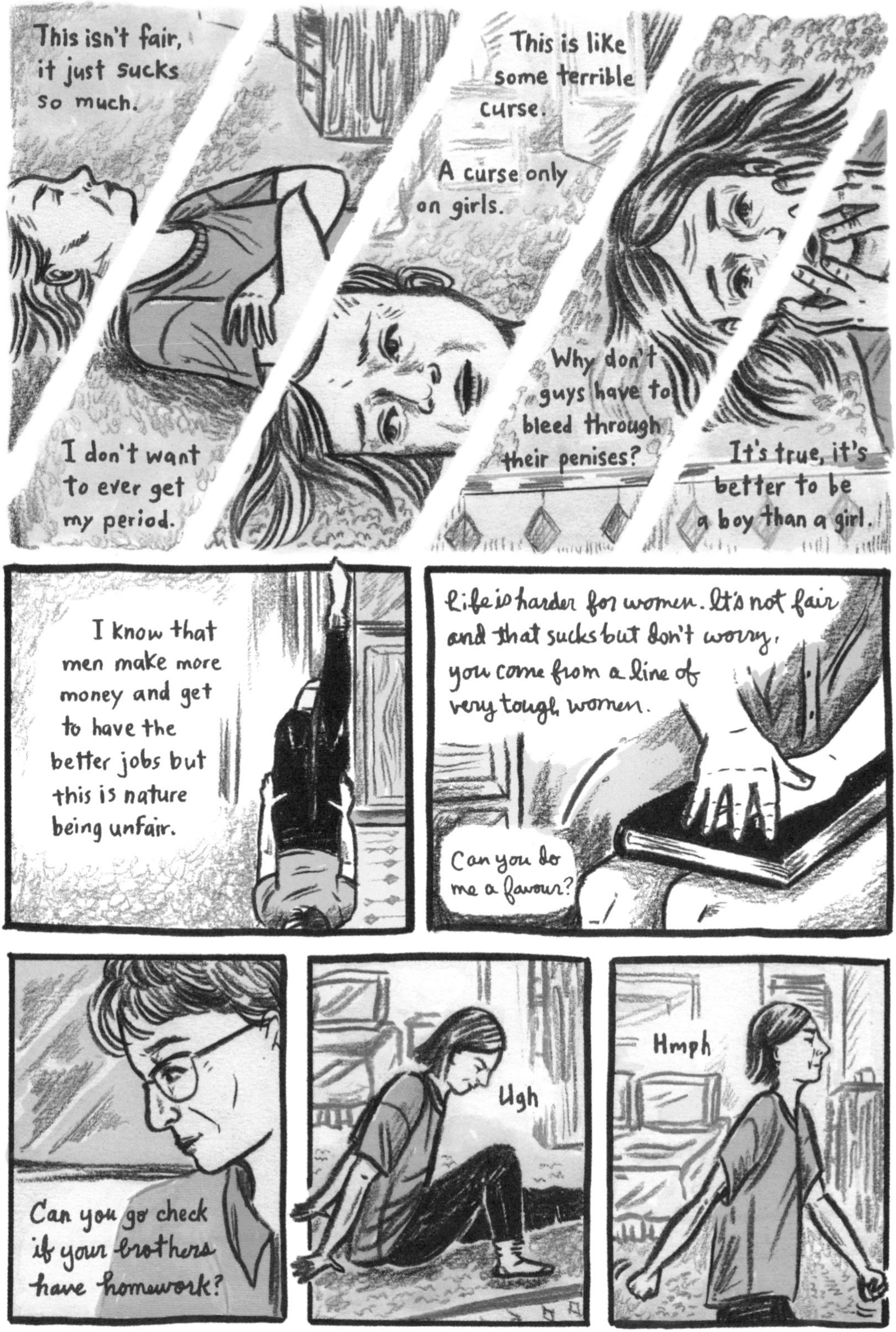
This isn't fair, it just sucks so much.
I don't want to ever get my period.
This is like some terrible curse.
A curse only on girls.
Why don't guys have to bleed through their penises?
It's true, it's better to be a boy than a girl.
I know that men make more money and get to have the better jobs but this is nature being unfair.
Life is harder for women. It's not fair and that sucks but don't worry, you come from a line of very tough women.
Can you do me a favour?
Can you go check if your brothers have homework?
Ugh
Hmph

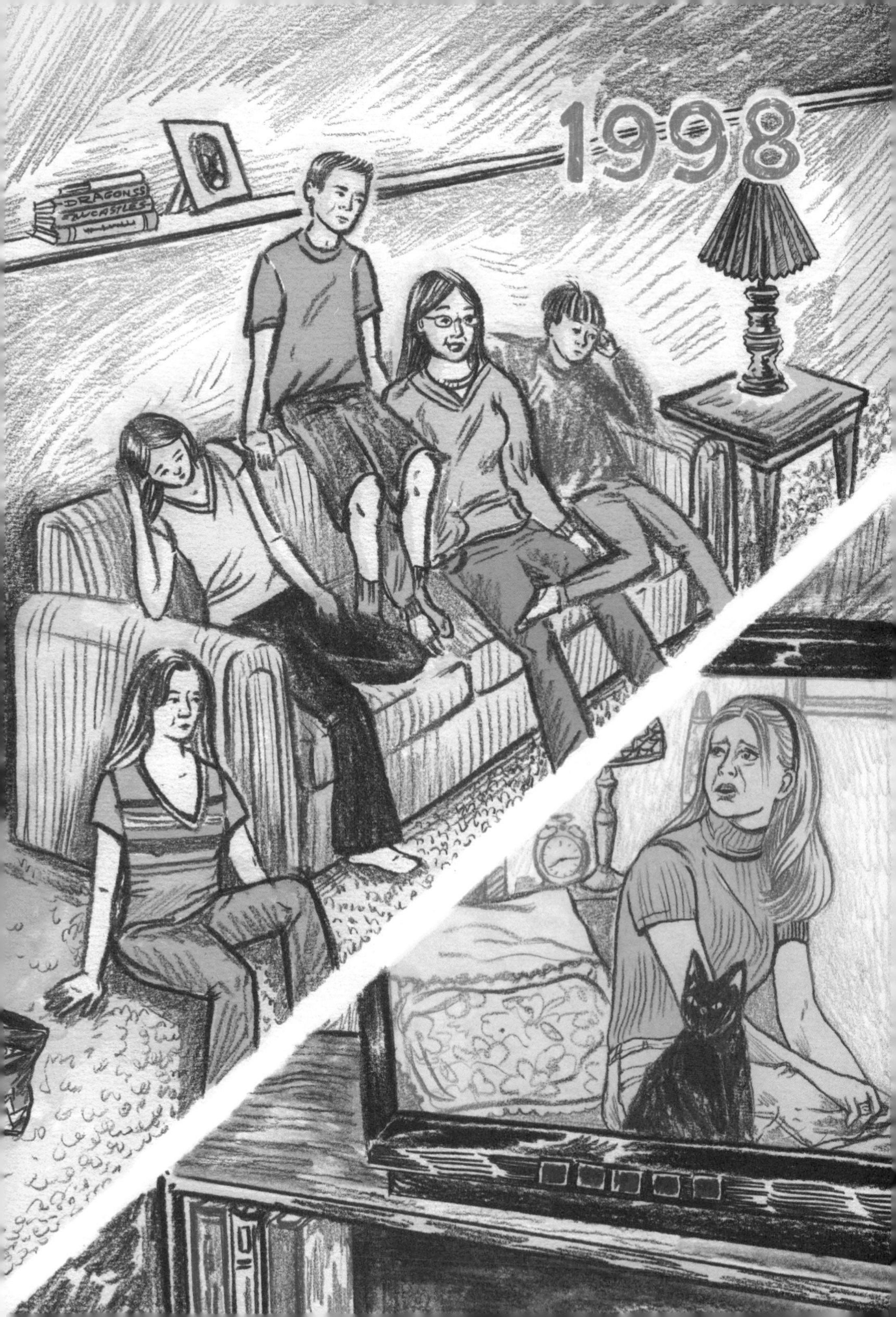
1998
DRAGONS
CASTLES

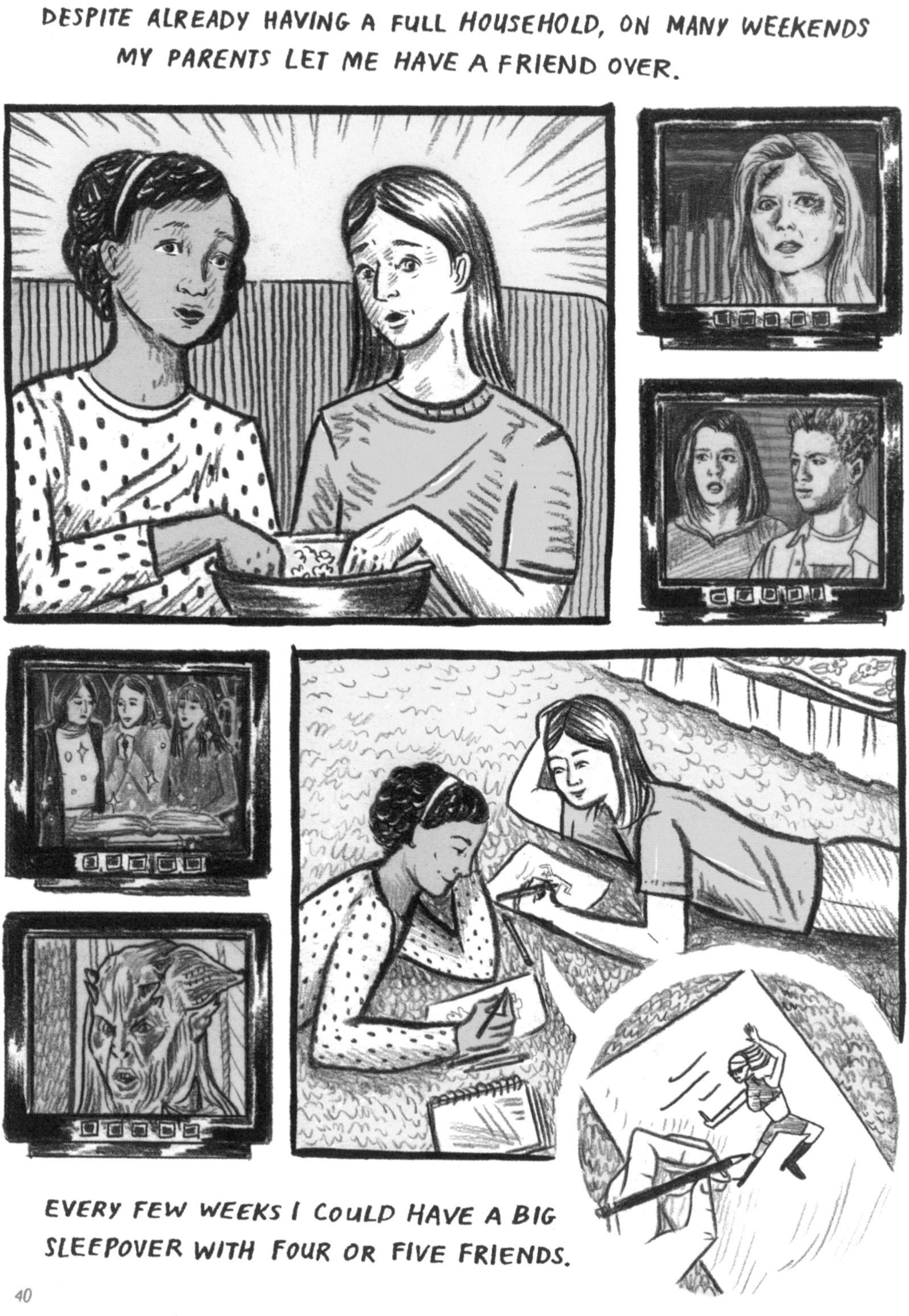
DESPITE ALREADY HAVING A FULL HOUSEHOLD, ON MANY WEEKENDS MY PARENTS LET ME HAVE A FRIEND OVER.
EVERY FEW WEEKS I COULD HAVE A BIG SLEEPOVER WITH FOUR OR FIVE FRIENDS.

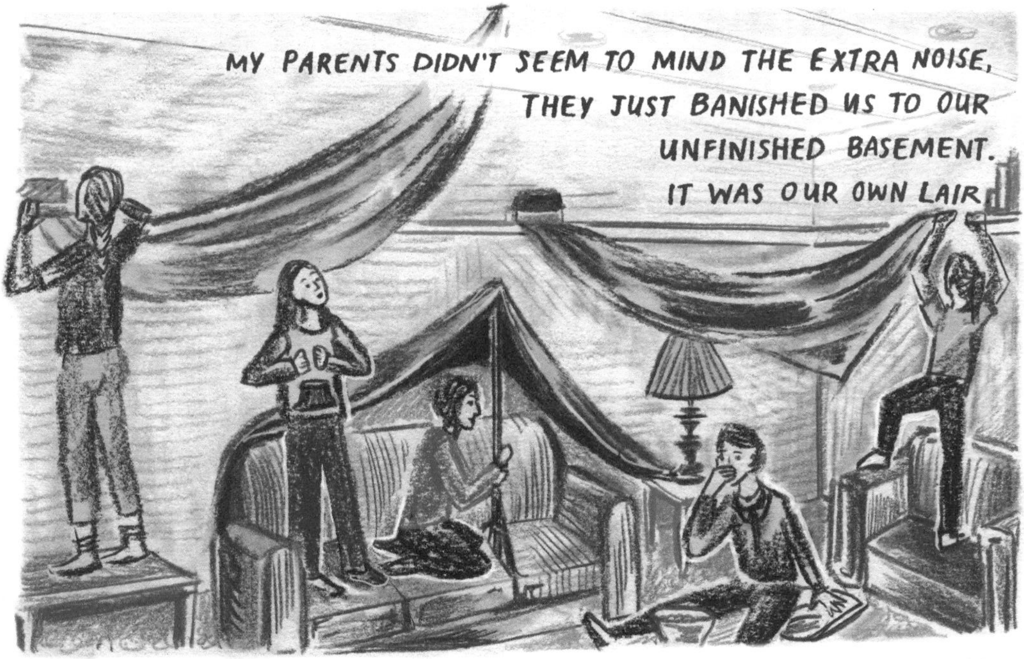
MY PARENTS DIDN'T SEEM TO MIND THE EXTRA NOISE, THEY JUST BANISHED US TO OUR UNFINISHED BASEMENT.
IT WAS OUR OWN LAIR.

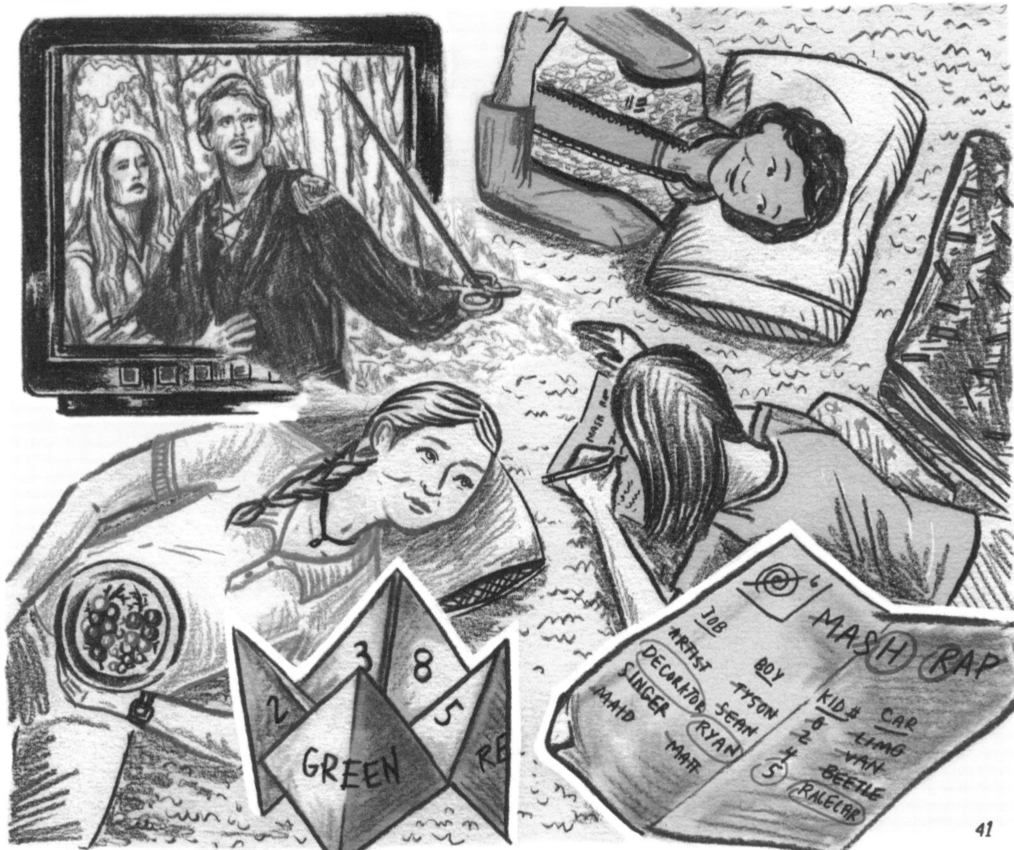
3
8
2
5
GREEN
MASH
RAP
JOB
ARTIST
DECORATOR
SINGER
MAID
BOY
TYSON
SEAN
RYAN
MATT
KID #
CAR
LIMO
VAN
BEETLE
RACECAR

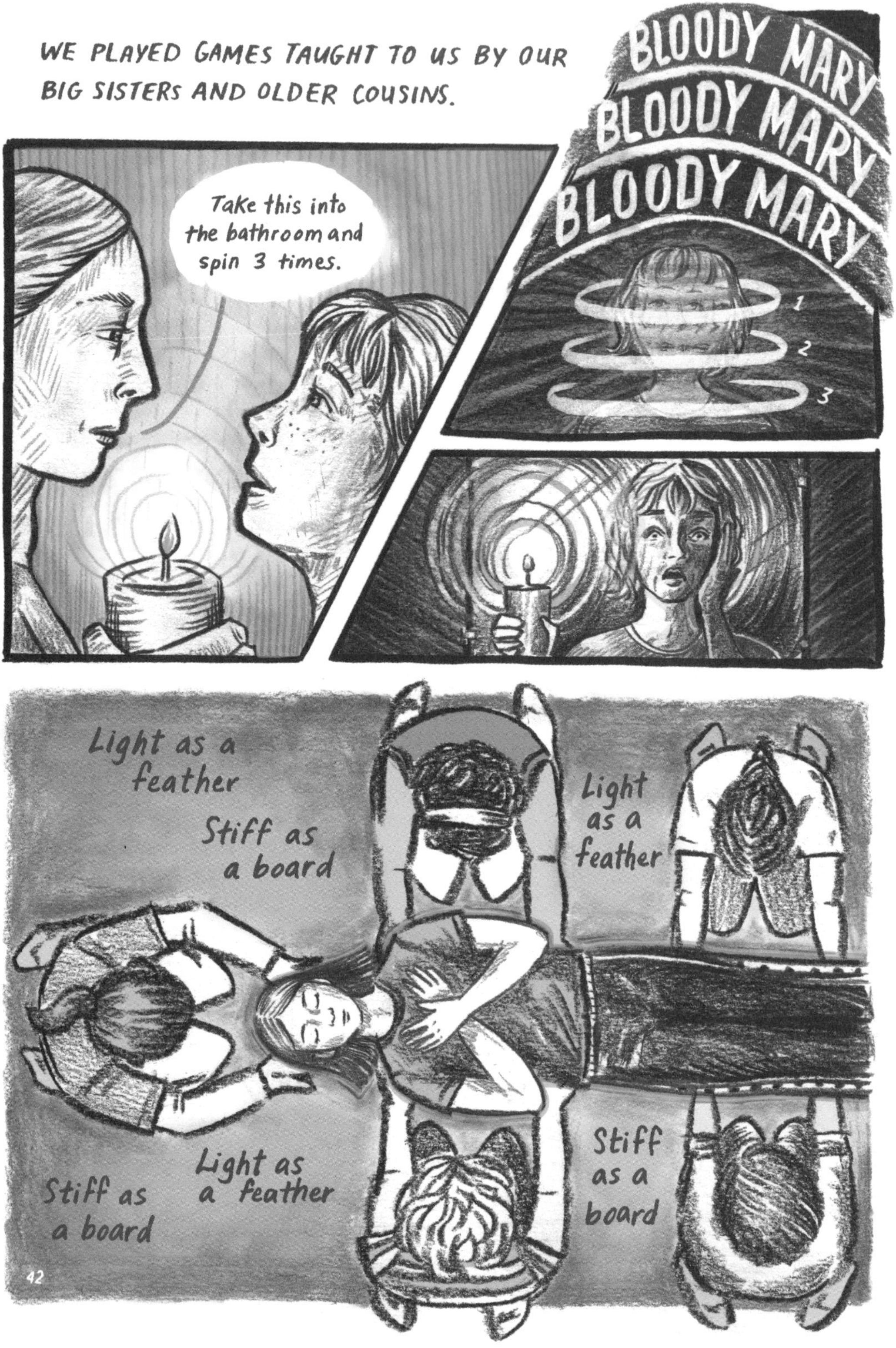
WE PLAYED GAMES TAUGHT TO US BY OUR BIG SISTERS AND OLDER COUSINS.
Take this into the bathroom and spin 3 times.
BLOODY MARY
BLOODY MARY
BLOODY MARY
1
2
3
Light as a feather
Stiff as a board
Light as a feather
Stiff as a board
Light as a feather
Stiff as a board

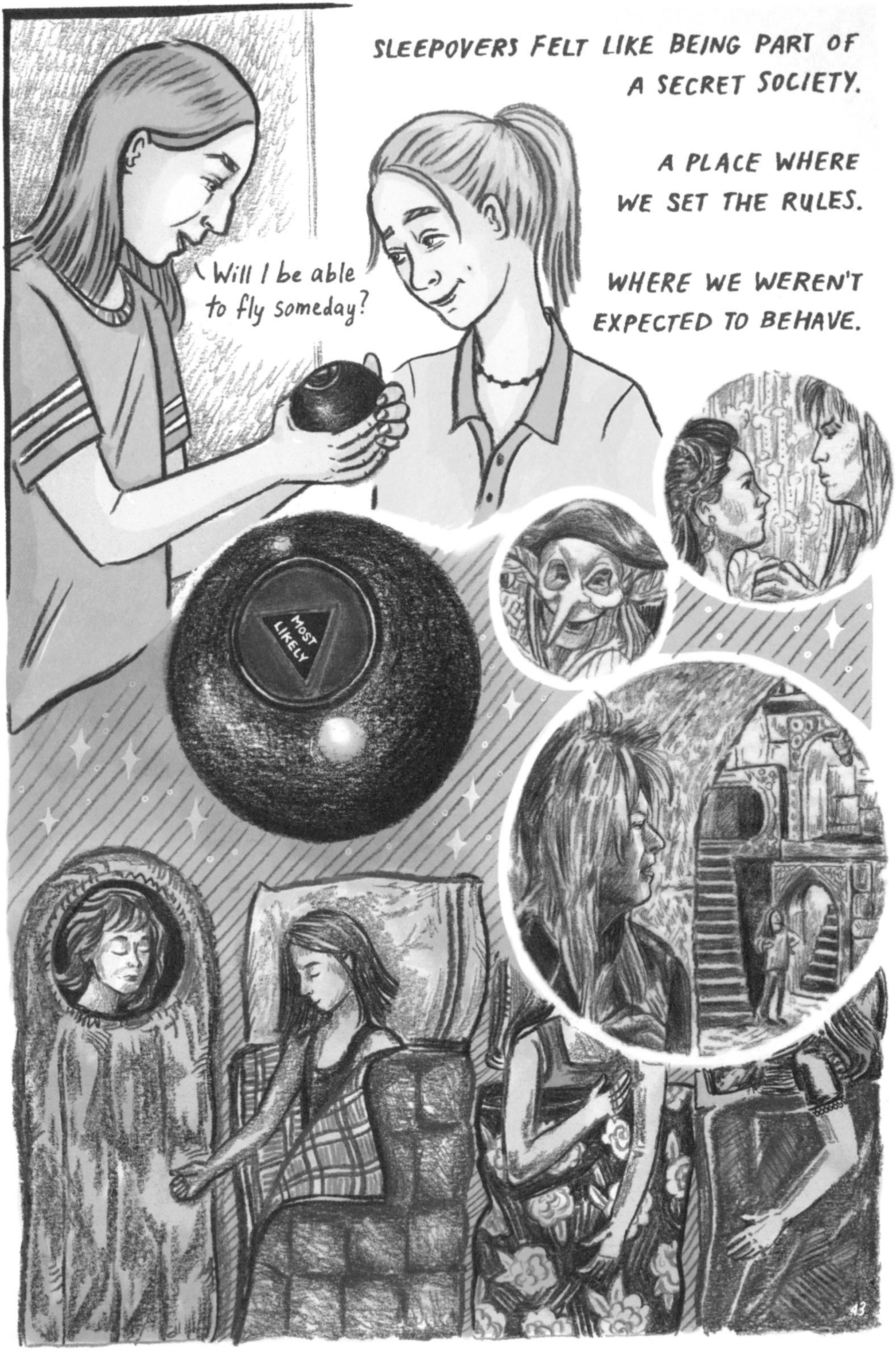
SLEEPOVERS FELT LIKE BEING PART OF A SECRET SOCIETY.
A PLACE WHERE WE SET THE RULES.
WHERE WE WEREN'T EXPECTED TO BEHAVE.
Will I be able to fly someday?
MOST LIKELY

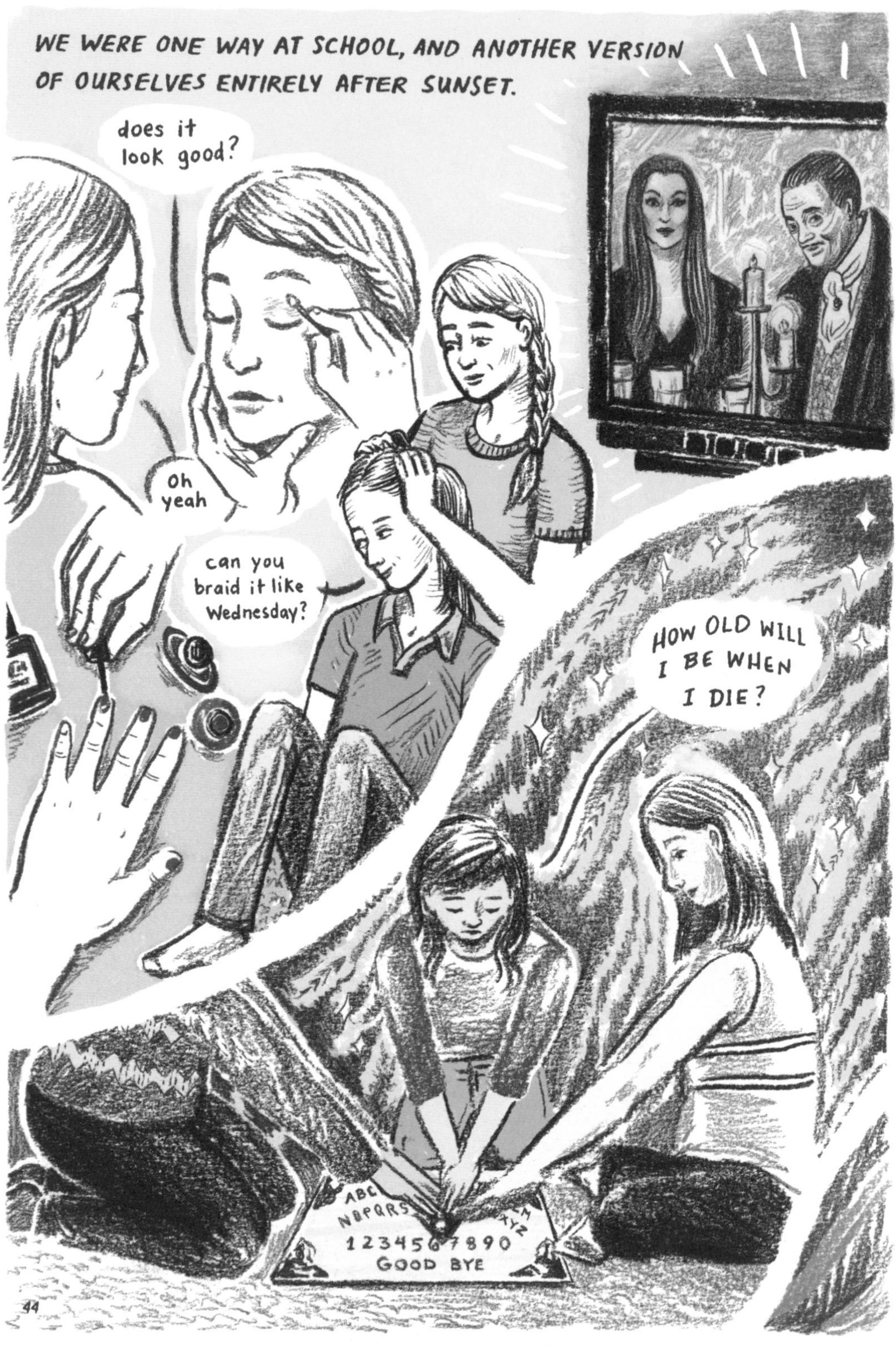
WE WERE ONE WAY AT SCHOOL, AND ANOTHER VERSION OF OURSELVES ENTIRELY AFTER SUNSET.
does it look good?
Oh yeah
can you braid it like Wednesday?
HOW OLD WILL I BE WHEN I DIE?
ABC
NOPQRS
XYZ
1234567890
GOOD BYE

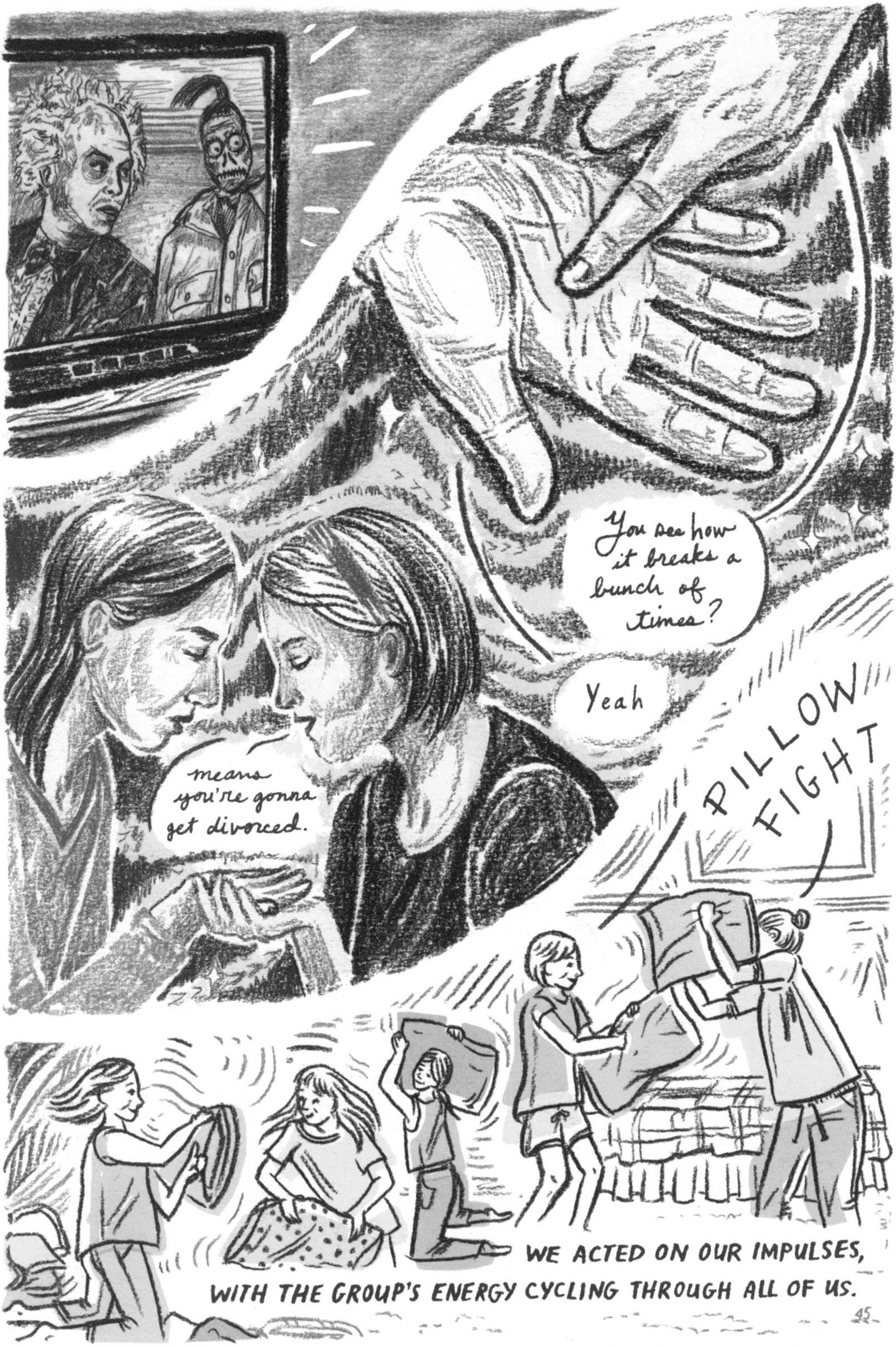
You see how it breaks a bunch of times?
Yeah
means you're gonna get divorced.
PILLOW FIGHT
WE ACTED ON OUR IMPULSES,
WITH THE GROUP'S ENERGY CYCLING THROUGH ALL OF US.

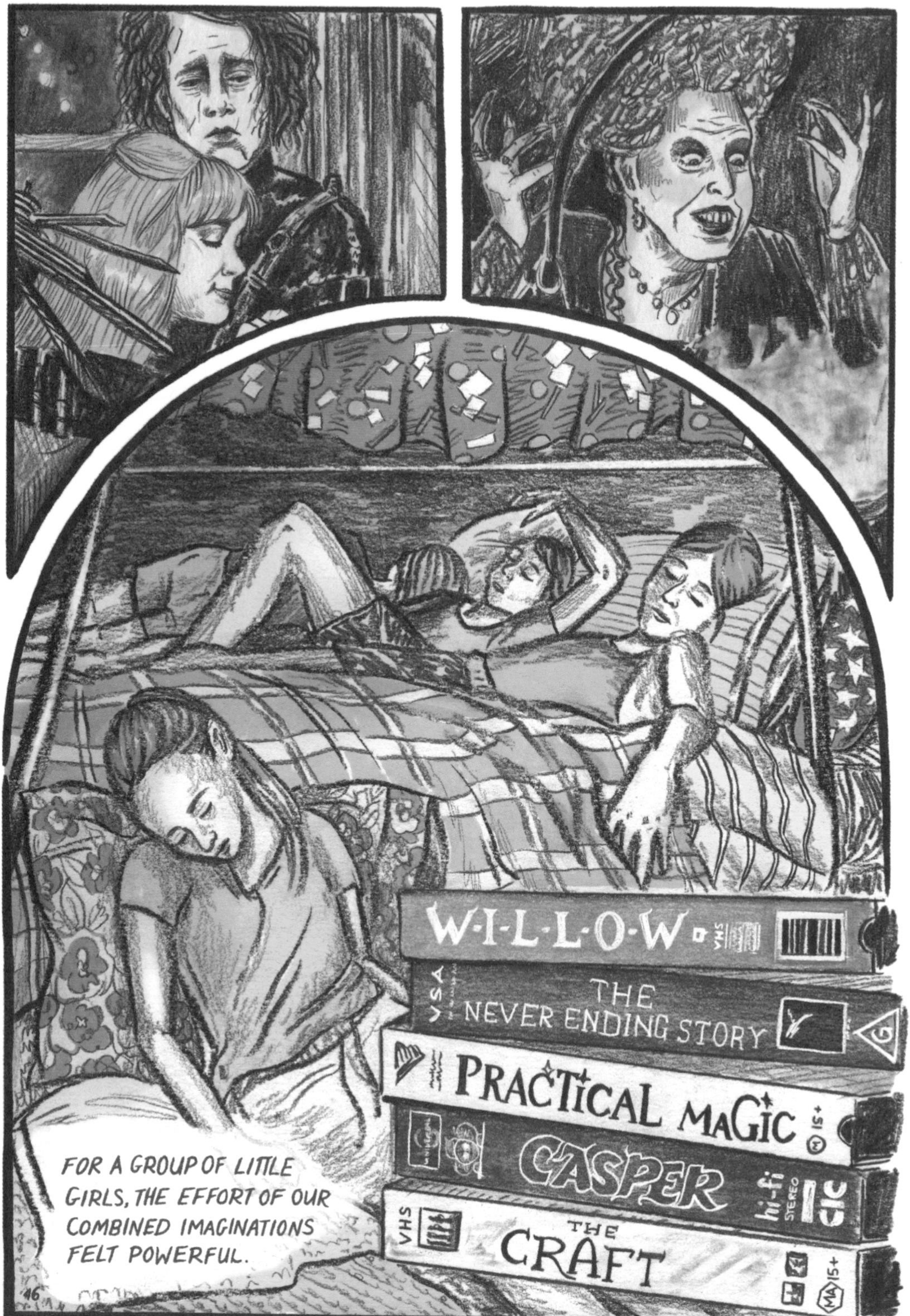
W·I·L·L·O·W
VHS
THE NEVER ENDING STORY
PRACTICAL MAGIC
15+
CASPER
hi-fi STEREO
VHS
THE CRAFT
MA 15+
FOR A GROUP OF LITTLE GIRLS, THE EFFORT OF OUR COMBINED IMAGINATIONS FELT POWERFUL.

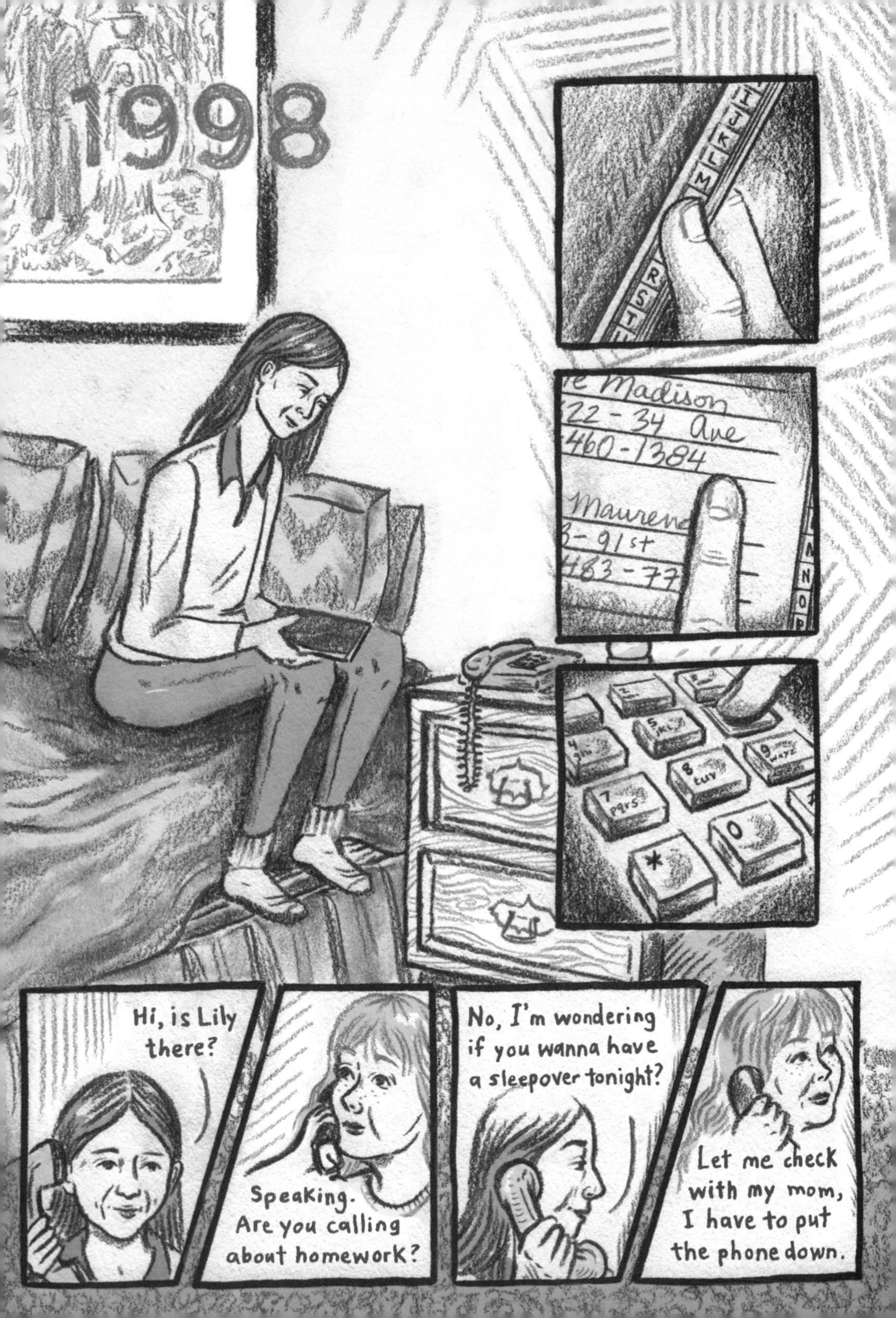
1998
Madison
22 - 34 Ave
460-1384
Maurene
3-91st
483-77
Hi, is Lily there?
Speaking. Are you calling about homework?
No, I'm wondering if you wanna have a sleepover tonight?
Let me check with my mom, I have to put the phone down.

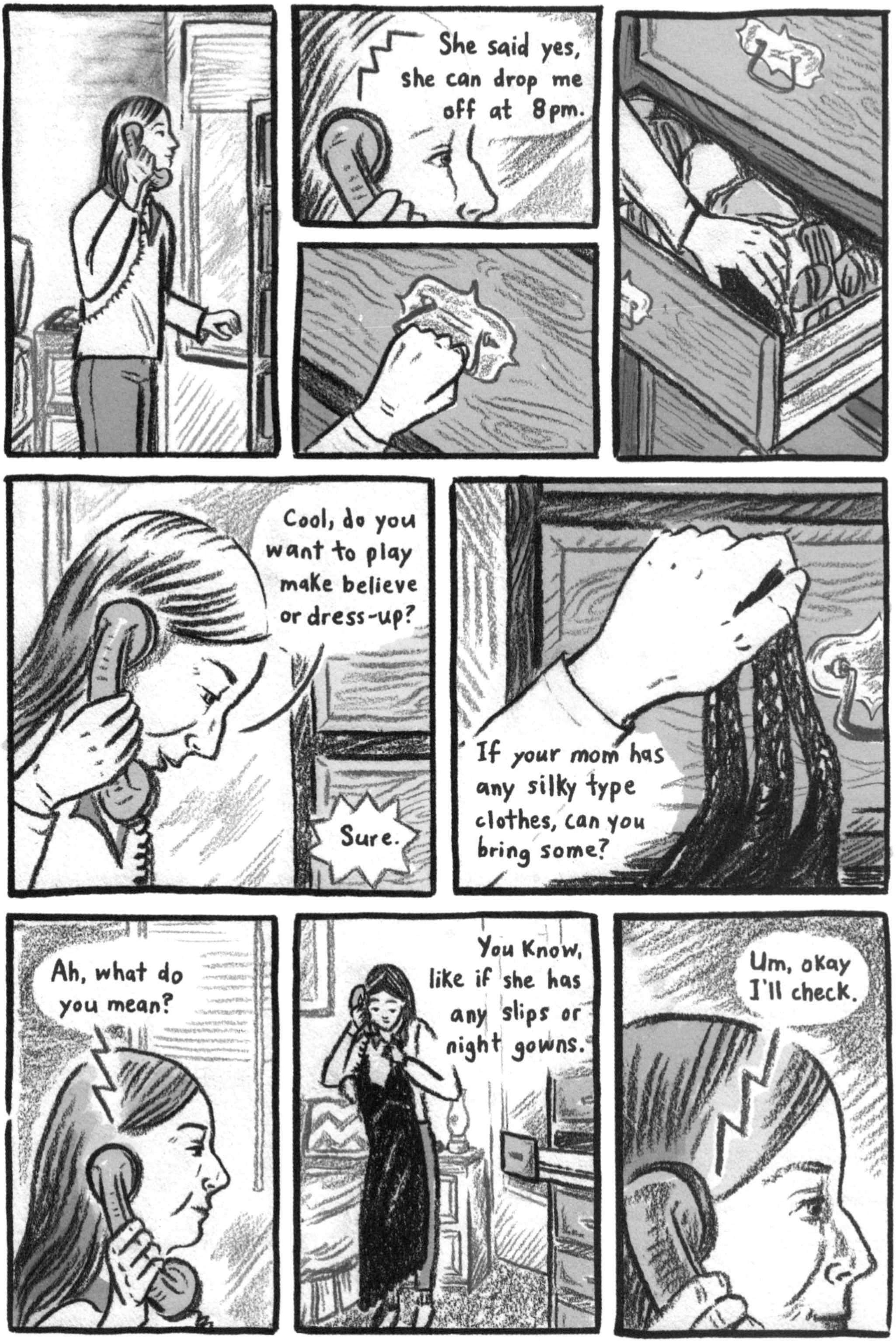
She said yes, she can drop me off at 8pm.
Cool, do you want to play make believe or dress-up?
Sure.
If your mom has any silky type clothes, can you bring some?
Ah, what do you mean?
You know, like if she has any slips or night gowns.
Um, okay I'll check.

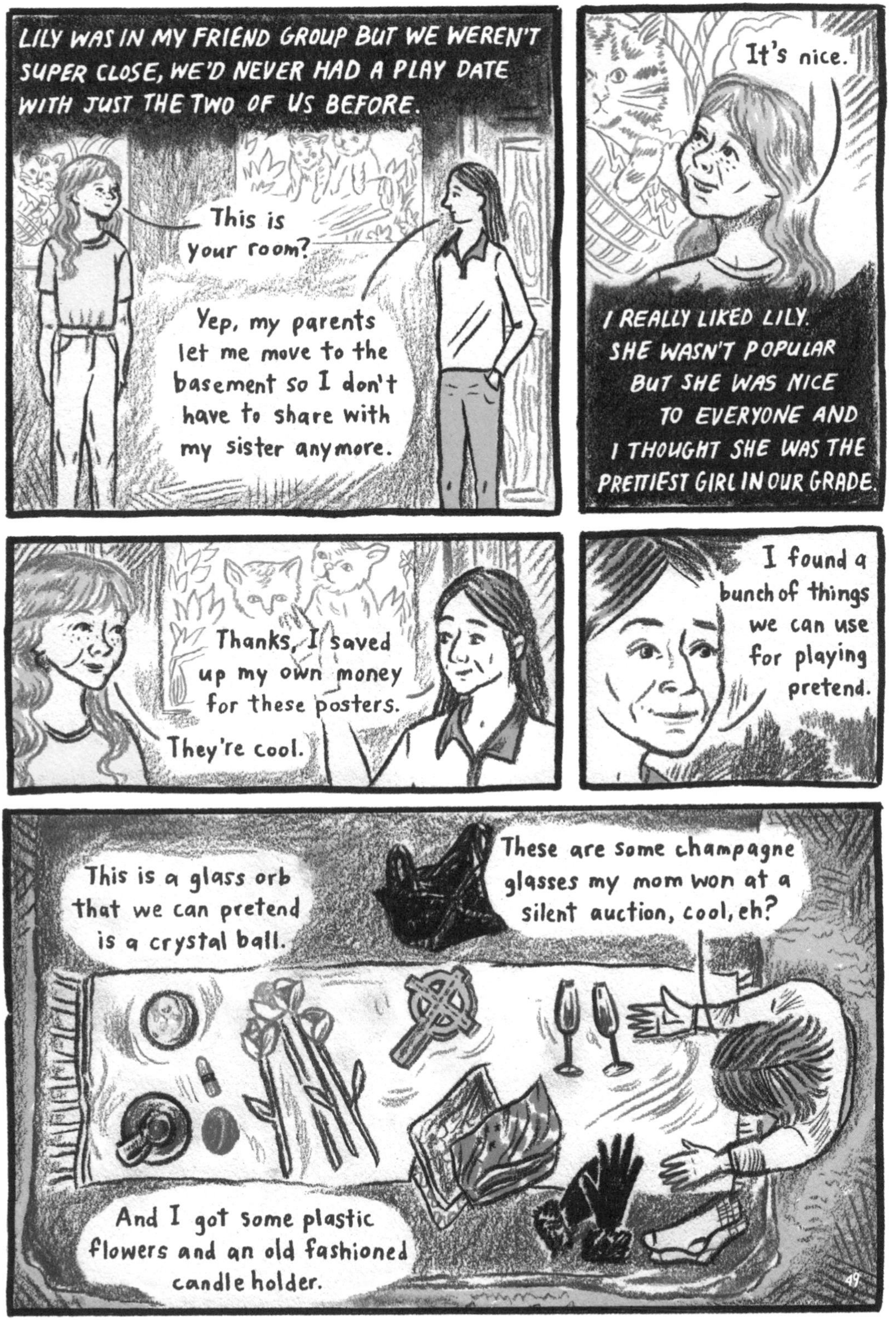
LILY WAS IN MY FRIEND GROUP BUT WE WEREN'T SUPER CLOSE, WE'D NEVER HAD A PLAY DATE WITH JUST THE TWO OF US BEFORE.
This is your room?
Yep, my parents let me move to the basement so I don't have to share with my sister anymore.
It's nice.
I REALLY LIKED LILY. SHE WASN'T POPULAR BUT SHE WAS NICE TO EVERYONE AND I THOUGHT SHE WAS THE PRETTIEST GIRL IN OUR GRADE.
Thanks, I saved up my own money for these posters.
They're cool.
I found a bunch of things we can use for playing pretend.
This is a glass orb that we can pretend is a crystal ball.
These are some champagne glasses my mom won at a silent auction, cool, eh?
And I got some plastic flowers and an old fashioned candle holder.
49

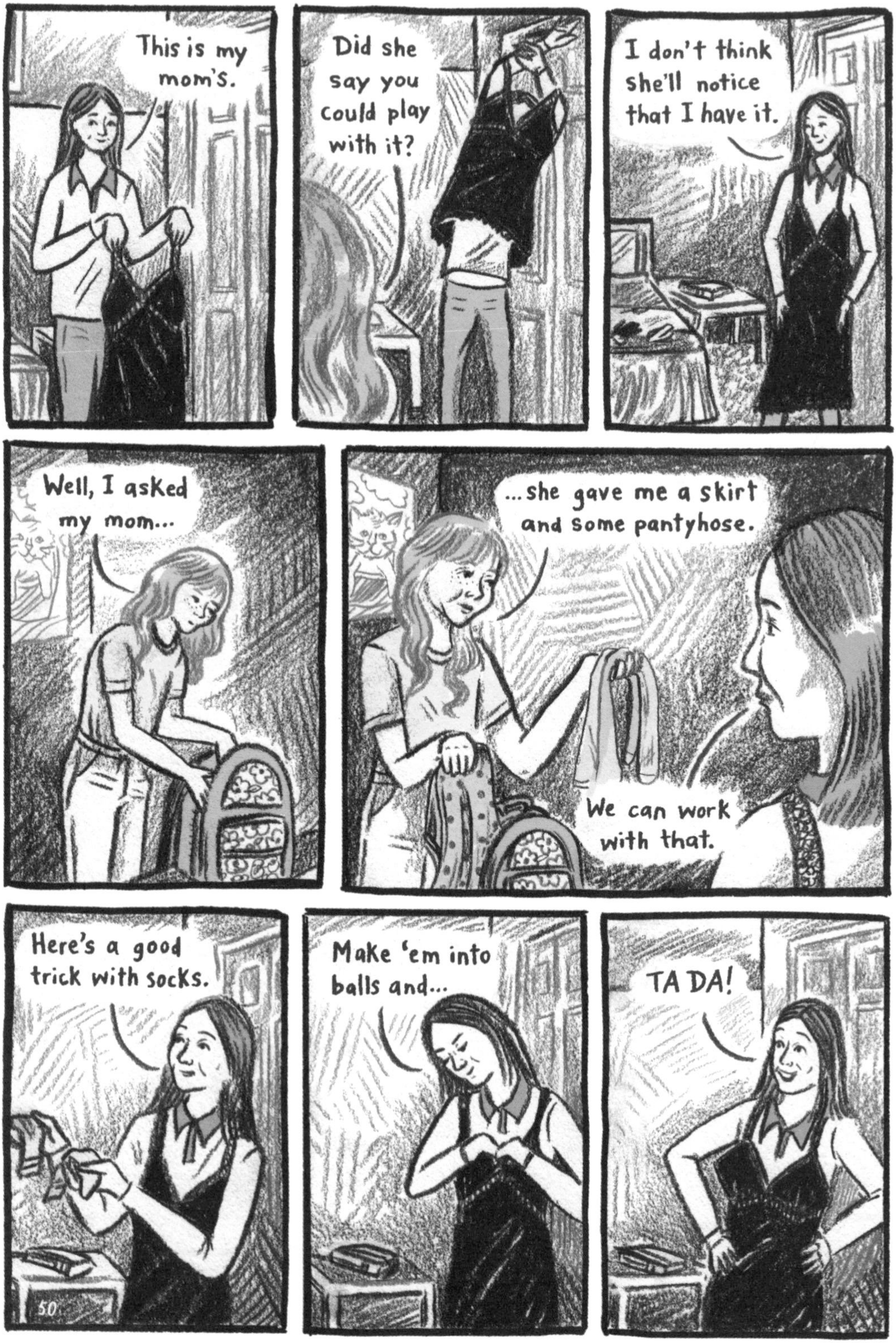
This is my mom's.
Did she say you could play with it?
I don't think she'll notice that I have it.
Well, I asked my mom...
...she gave me a skirt and some pantyhose.
We can work with that.
Here's a good trick with socks.
Make 'em into balls and...
TA DA!

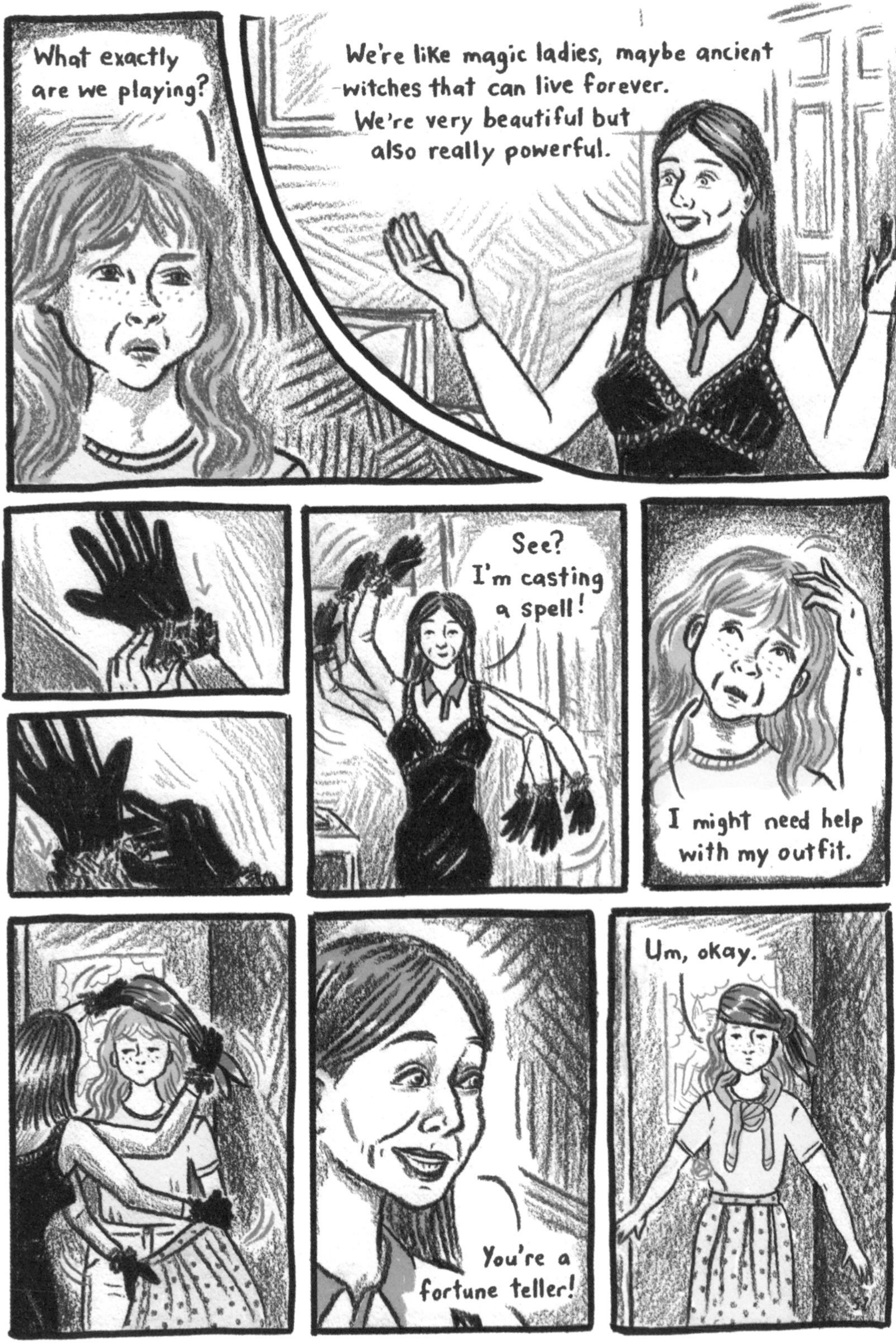
What exactly are we playing?
We're like magic ladies, maybe ancient witches that can live forever. We're very beautiful but also really powerful.
See? I'm casting a spell!
I might need help with my outfit.
You're a fortune teller!
Um, okay.

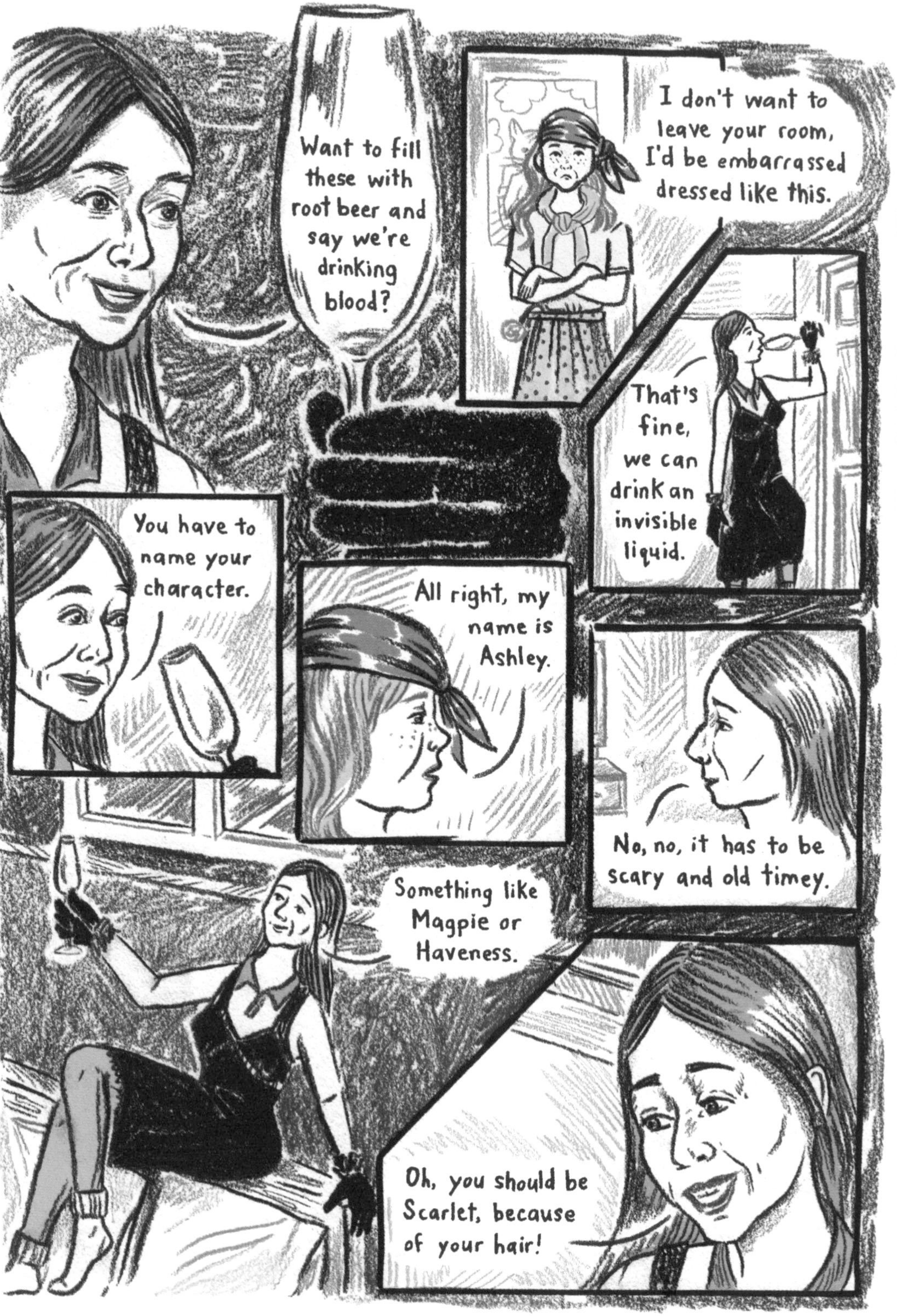
Want to fill these with root beer and say we're drinking blood?
I don't want to leave your room, I'd be embarrassed dressed like this.
That's fine, we can drink an invisible liquid.
You have to name your character.
All right, my name is Ashley.
No, no, it has to be scary and old timey.
Something like Magpie or Haveness.
Oh, you should be Scarlet, because of your hair!

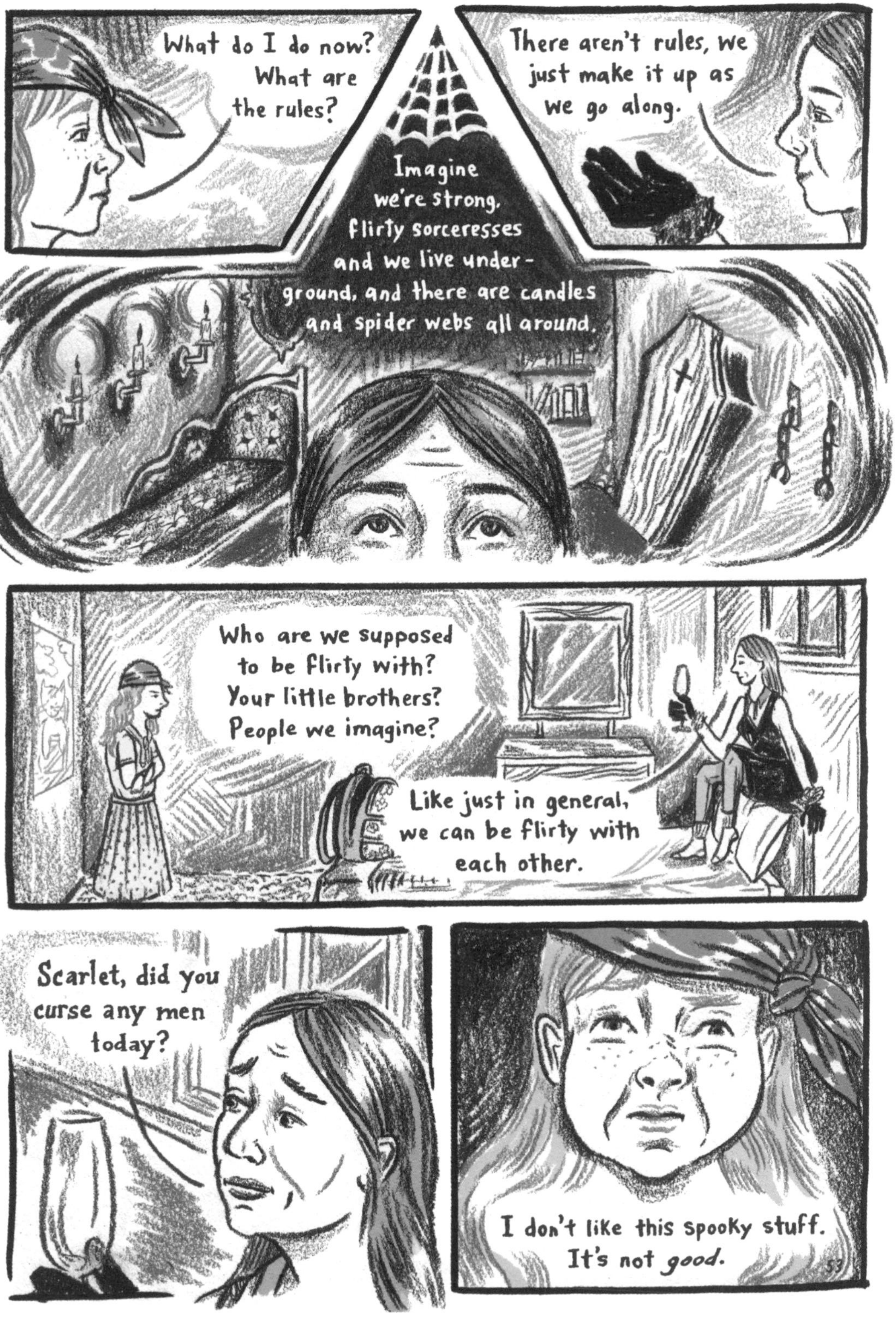
What do I do now? What are the rules?
There aren't rules, we just make it up as we go along.
Imagine we're strong, flirty sorceresses and we live under-ground, and there are candles and spider webs all around.
Who are we supposed to be flirty with? Your little brothers? People we imagine?
Like just in general, we can be flirty with each other.
Scarlet, did you curse any men today?
I don't like this spooky stuff. It's not *good*.

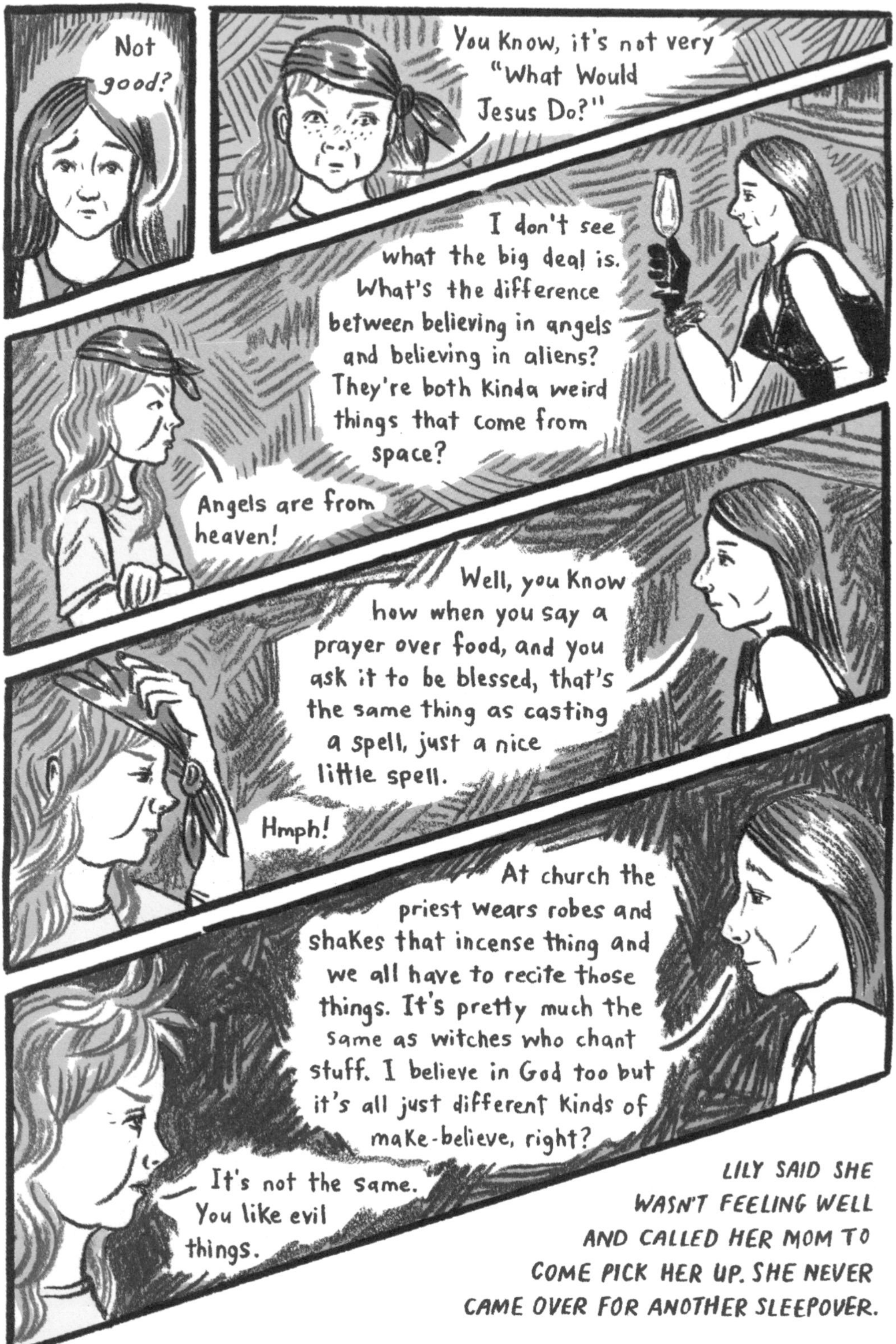

Not good?
You know, it's not very "What Would Jesus Do?"
I don't see what the big deal is. What's the difference between believing in angels and believing in aliens? They're both kinda weird things that come from space?
Angels are from heaven!
Well, you know how when you say a prayer over food, and you ask it to be blessed, that's the same thing as casting a spell, just a nice little spell.
Hmph!
At church the priest wears robes and shakes that incense thing and we all have to recite those things. It's pretty much the same as witches who chant stuff. I believe in God too but it's all just different kinds of make-believe, right?
It's not the same. You like evil things.
LILY SAID SHE WASN'T FEELING WELL AND CALLED HER MOM TO COME PICK HER UP. SHE NEVER CAME OVER FOR ANOTHER SLEEPOVER.

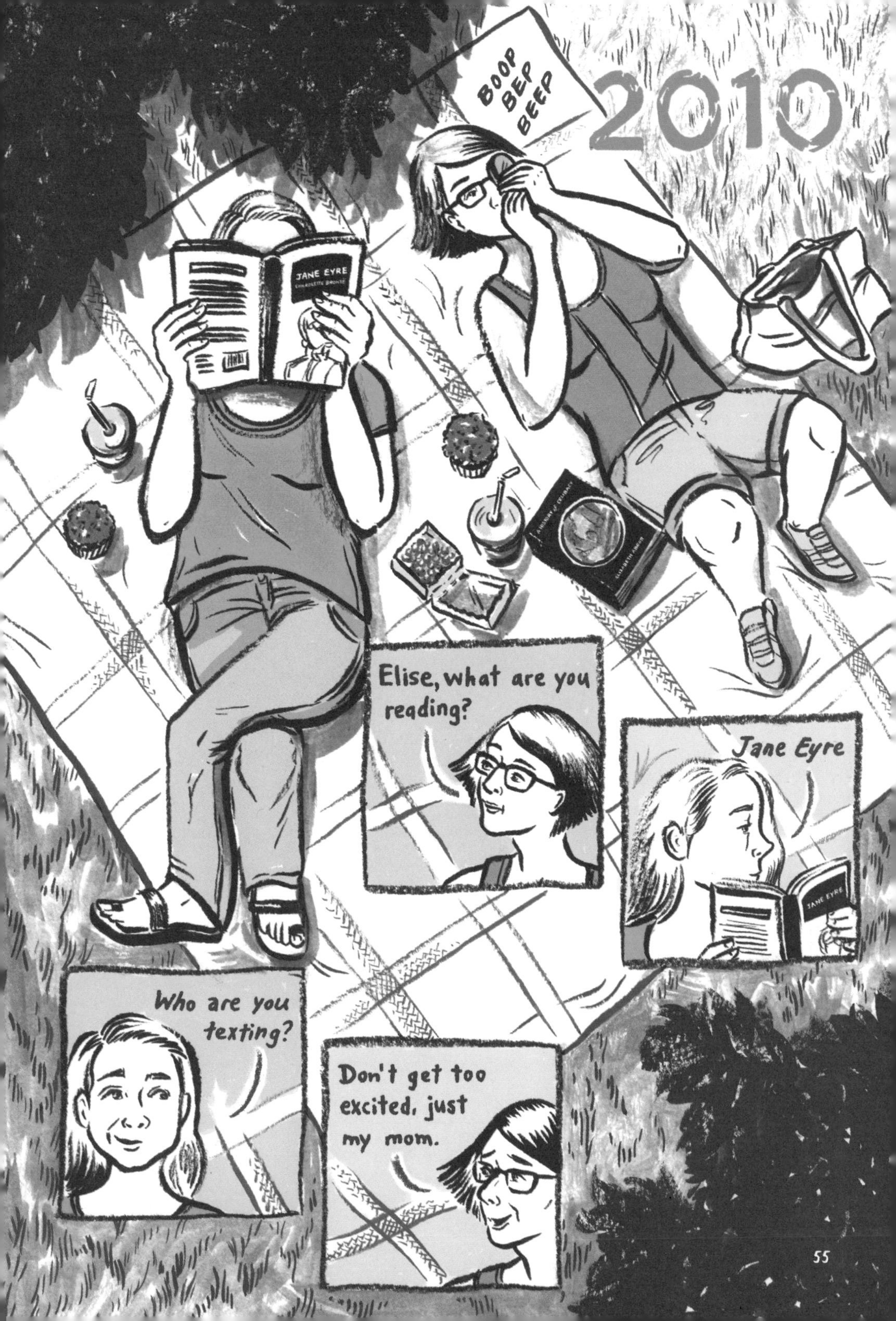
2010
BOOP BEP BEEP
JANE EYRE
Elise, what are you reading?
Jane Eyre
Who are you texting?
Don't get too excited, just my mom.

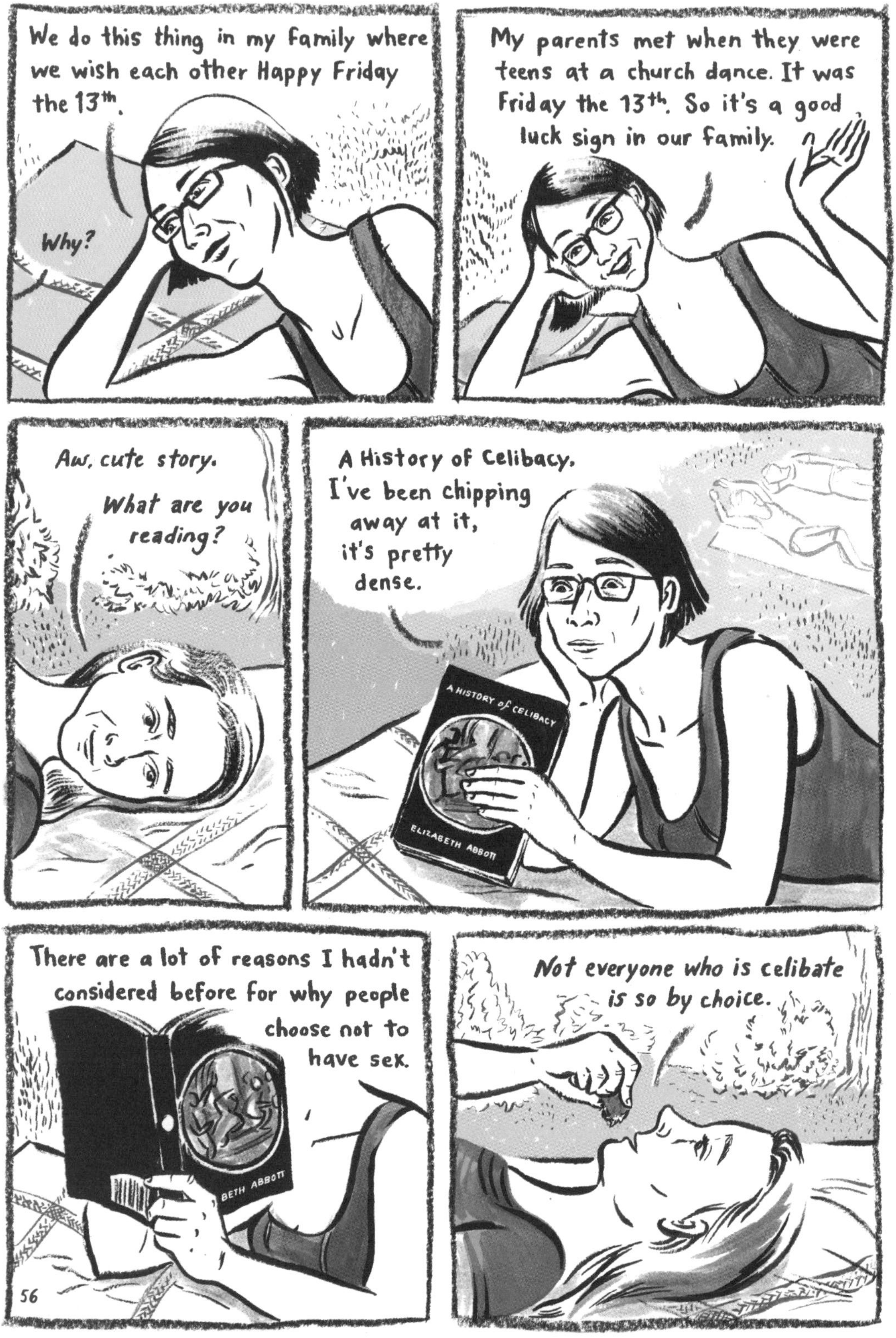
We do this thing in my family where we wish each other Happy Friday the 13th.
Why?
My parents met when they were teens at a church dance. It was Friday the 13th. So it's a good luck sign in our family.
Aw, cute story.
What are you reading?
A History of Celibacy. I've been chipping away at it, it's pretty dense.
A HISTORY of CELIBACY
ELIZABETH ABBOTT
There are a lot of reasons I hadn't considered before for why people choose not to have sex.
BETH ABBOTT
Not everyone who is celibate is so by choice.

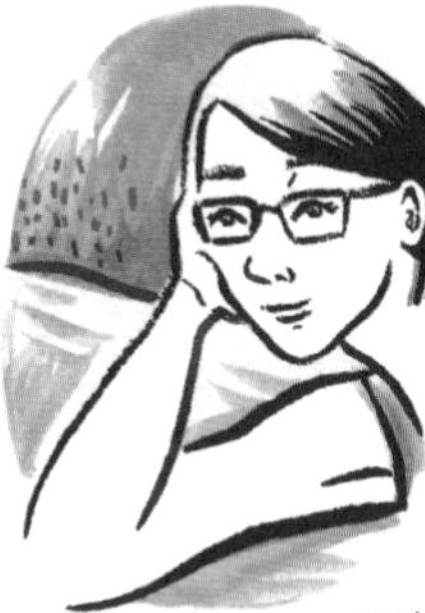

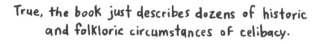

True, the book just describes dozens of historic and folkloric circumstances of celibacy.

In Greek mythology, there were no chaste Gods except for three virgin Goddesses, who recognized that if they wanted to rule their own lives, they could never give themselves to any man.

Athena the Goddess of War and Artemis the Goddess of Hunting enjoyed the same privileges as male Gods, while Hestia the Goddess of the Hearth and Family focused solely on keeping the flames of Mount Olympus alive.

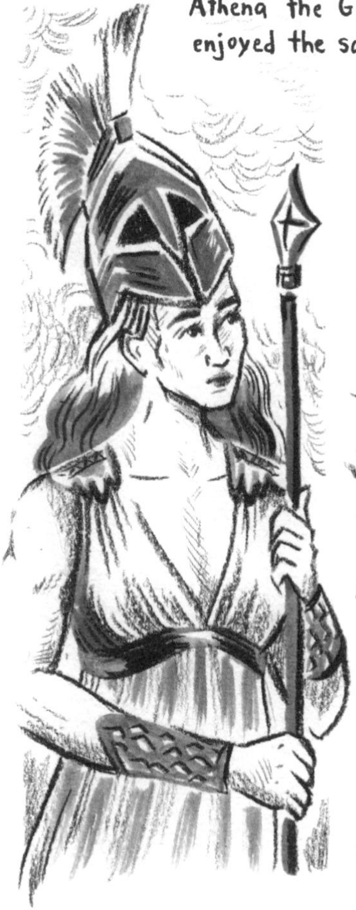

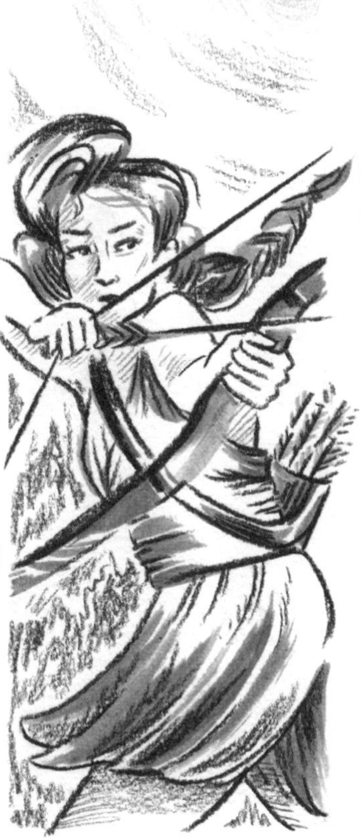

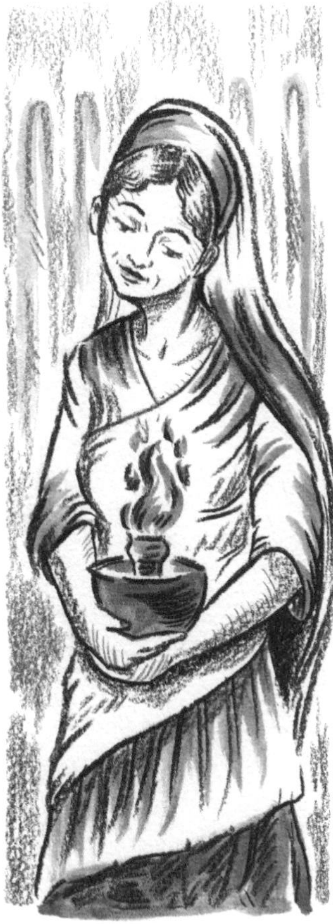

They turned away admirers and defended themselves against rape.

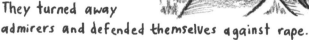

The Goddesses were important idols to Greek women who weren't citizens but the property of their fathers and husbands. When a woman adamantly refused to marry, Socrates' advice was to *set her to work like the slaves.*

One of the most well-known celibate historic figures was Queen Elizabeth I. In 1558, for her coronation she wore her long red hair down and unadorned to signify her virginity.

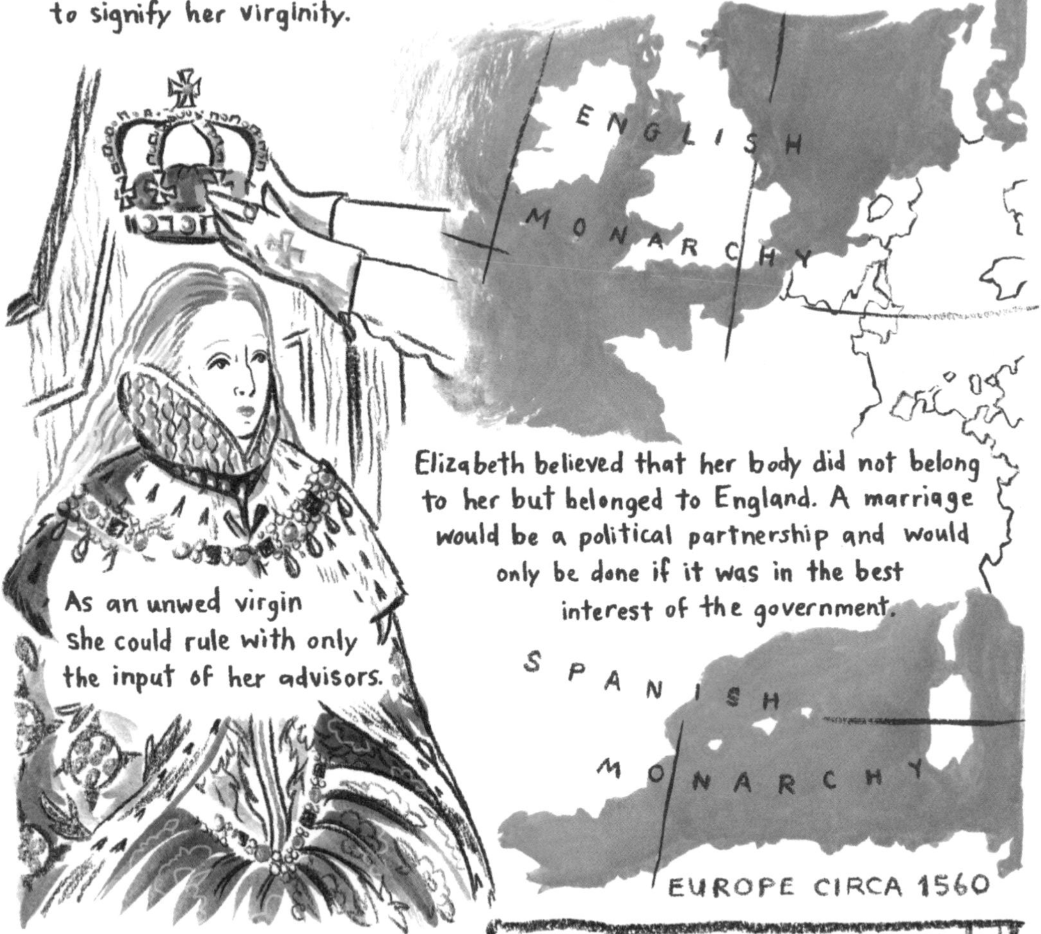
ENGLISH MONARCHY
Elizabeth believed that her body did not belong to her but belonged to England. A marriage would be a political partnership and would only be done if it was in the best interest of the government.
As an unwed virgin she could rule with only the input of her advisors.
SPANISH MONARCHY
EUROPE CIRCA 1560

Elizabeth cleverly used her singlehood as a political tool. She welcomed potential suitors and outwardly seemed open to marriage. Foreign suitors refrained from initiating any conflict with England, in hopes that a marriage would eventually materialize.

Her reign was one of the most peaceful in England's history.

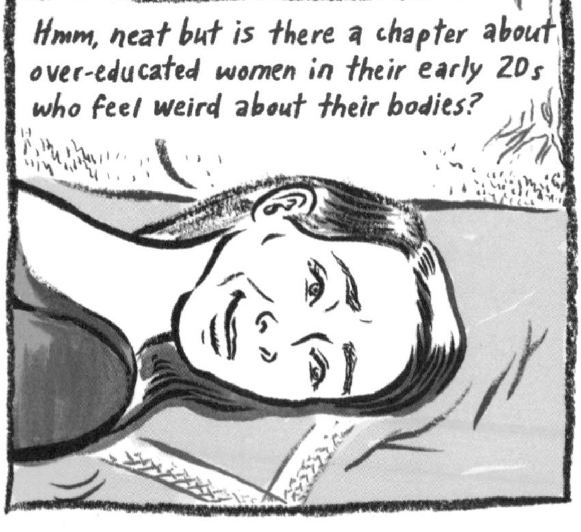
Hmm, neat but is there a chapter about over-educated women in their early 20s who feel weird about their bodies?

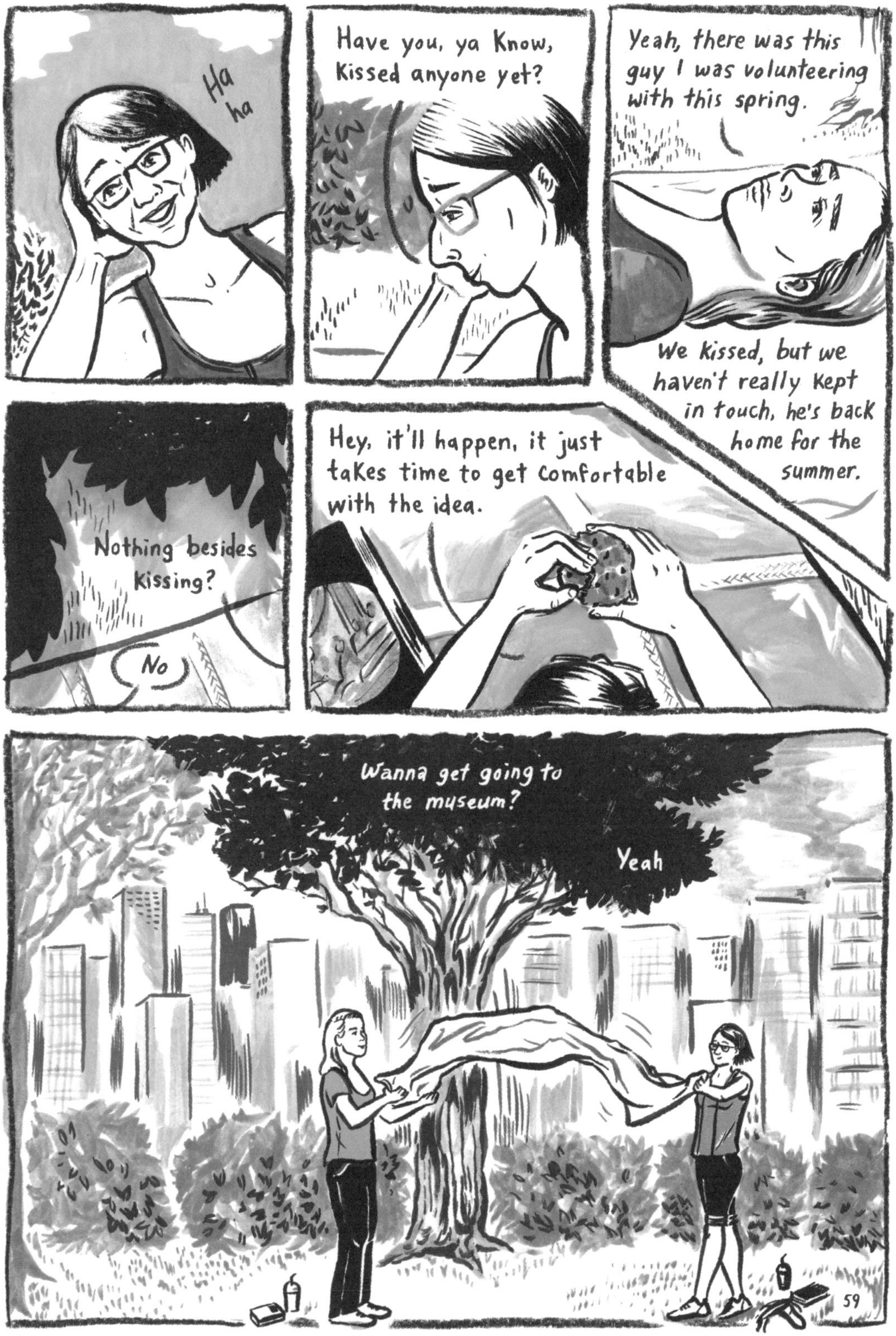
Ha ha
Have you, ya Know, Kissed anyone yet?
Yeah, there was this guy I was volunteering with this spring.
We kissed, but we haven't really Kept in touch, he's back home for the summer.
Nothing besides Kissing?
No
Hey, it'll happen, it just takes time to get comfortable with the idea.
Wanna get going to the museum?
Yeah

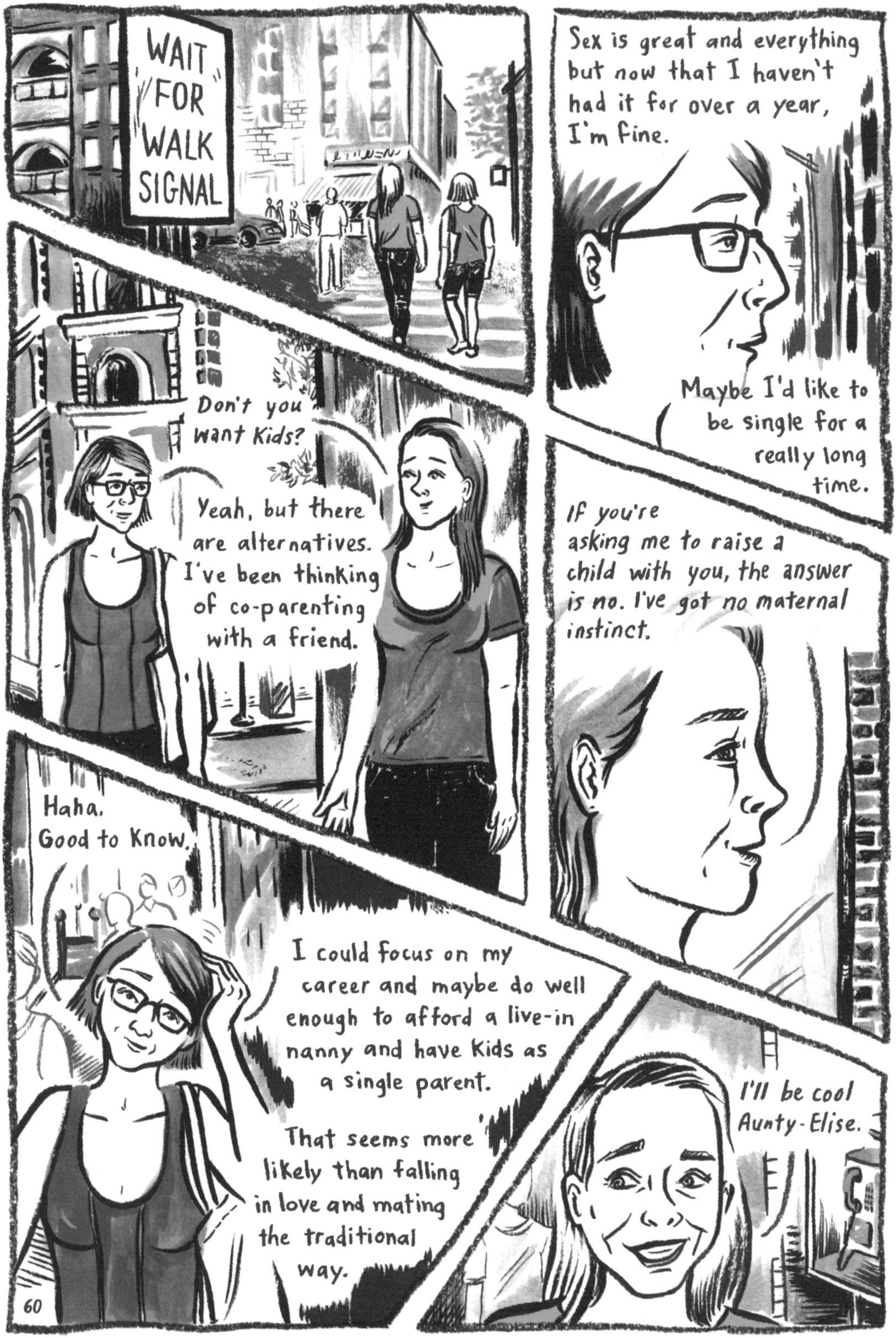

WAIT FOR WALK SIGNAL
Sex is great and everything but now that I haven't had it for over a year, I'm fine.
Maybe I'd like to be single for a really long time.
Don't you want Kids?
Yeah, but there are alternatives. I've been thinking of co-parenting with a friend.
If you're asking me to raise a child with you, the answer is no. I've got no maternal instinct.
Haha. Good to Know.
I could focus on my career and maybe do well enough to afford a live-in nanny and have Kids as a single parent.
That seems more likely than falling in love and mating the traditional way.
I'll be cool Aunty-Elise.

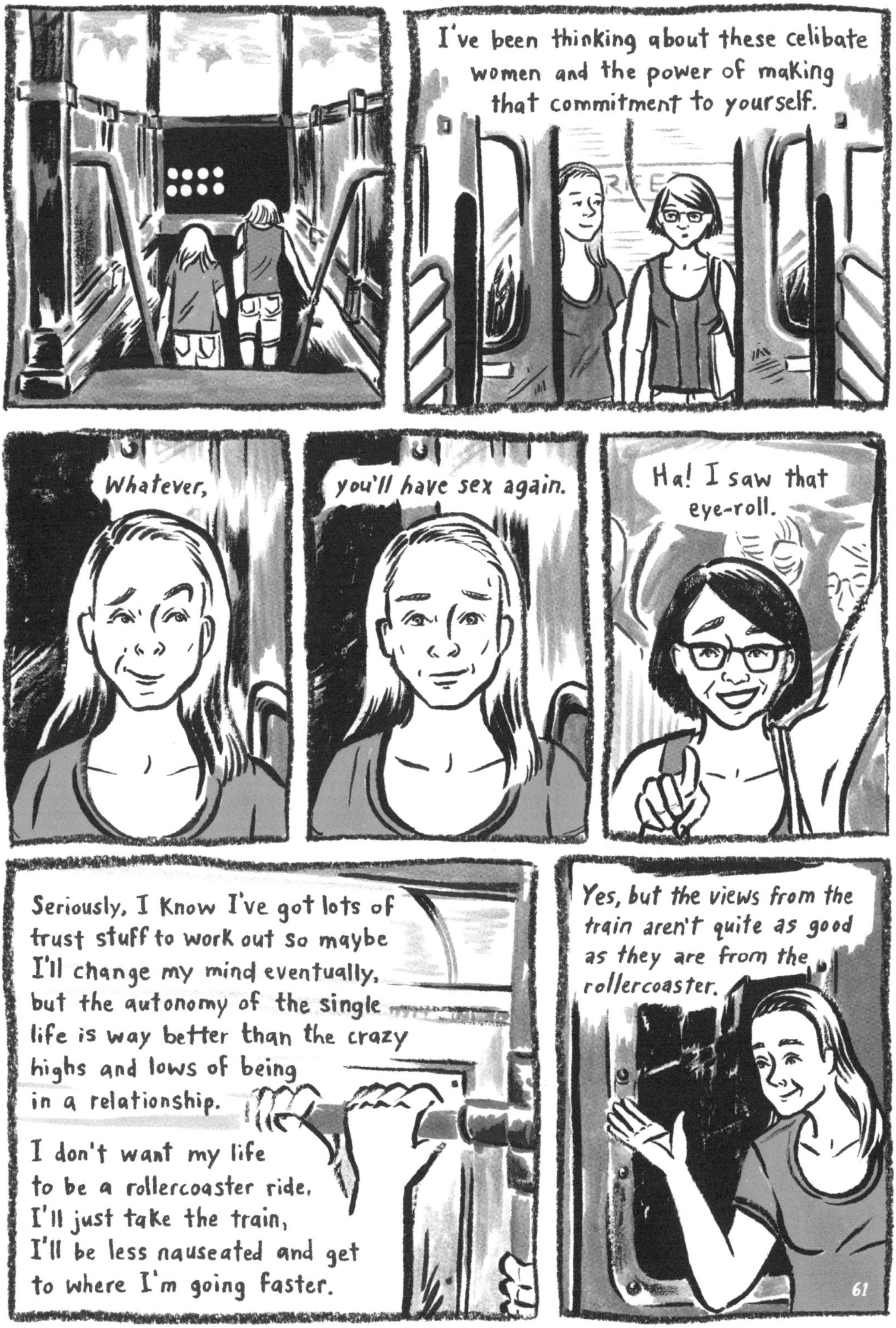
I've been thinking about these celibate women and the power of making that commitment to yourself.
Whatever,
you'll have sex again.
Ha! I saw that eye-roll.
Seriously, I know I've got lots of trust stuff to work out so maybe I'll change my mind eventually, but the autonomy of the single life is way better than the crazy highs and lows of being in a relationship.
I don't want my life to be a rollercoaster ride. I'll just take the train. I'll be less nauseated and get to where I'm going faster.
Yes, but the views from the train aren't quite as good as they are from the rollercoaster.

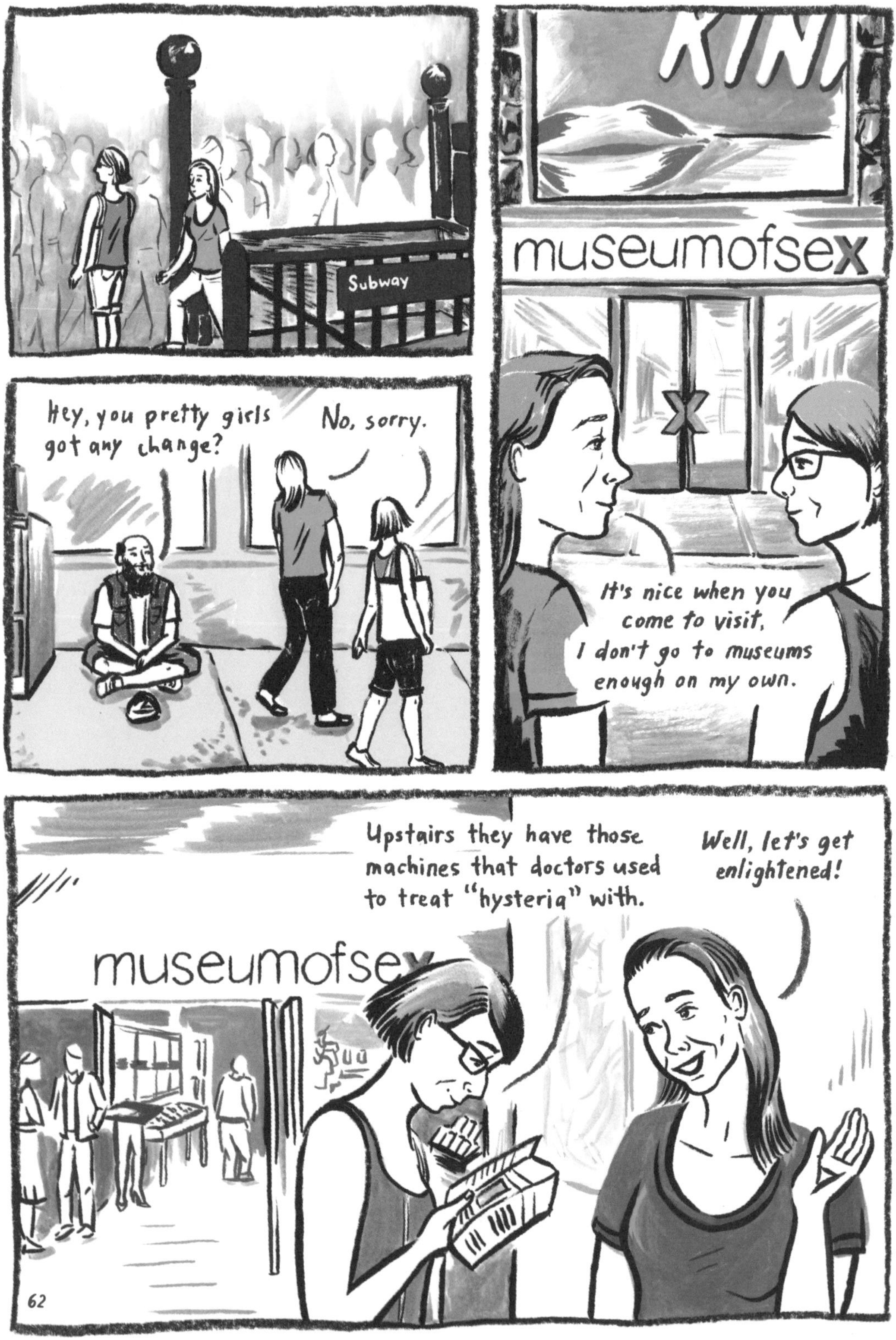
Subway
museumofsex
Hey, you pretty girls got any change?
No, sorry.
It's nice when you come to visit, I don't go to museums enough on my own.
museumofsex
Upstairs they have those machines that doctors used to treat "hysteria" with.
Well, let's get enlightened!

'99

'00

'01

I dreaded each day of junior high.
I'd started at a new, small, Catholic
school, equipped with a wardrobe
of hand-me-downs and two thick retainers
(one for the top and one for the bottom)
that gave me a tease-worthy lisp and
horrific smelling breath.

I had more bullies than friends and it felt like the
popular kids existed just to make me feel inferior.

I struggled through grade 7, feeling both ugly and stupid.
Thinking it was better to be pretty and smart,
by grade 8 I was determined to do something about
the half of those two things I felt I could control.

As a defensive mechanism, I focused hard on school
and vastly improved my grades.
Still, I wasn't happy there but I'd earned
some respect. I clutched on to my good grades like
a shield and wore my intelligence like armour.

In grade 9, I transferred to a liberal arts school where
I instantly felt like I had found my people.
Everyone was unique, everyone was accepting,
everyone thought it was cool that
I was good at drawing.

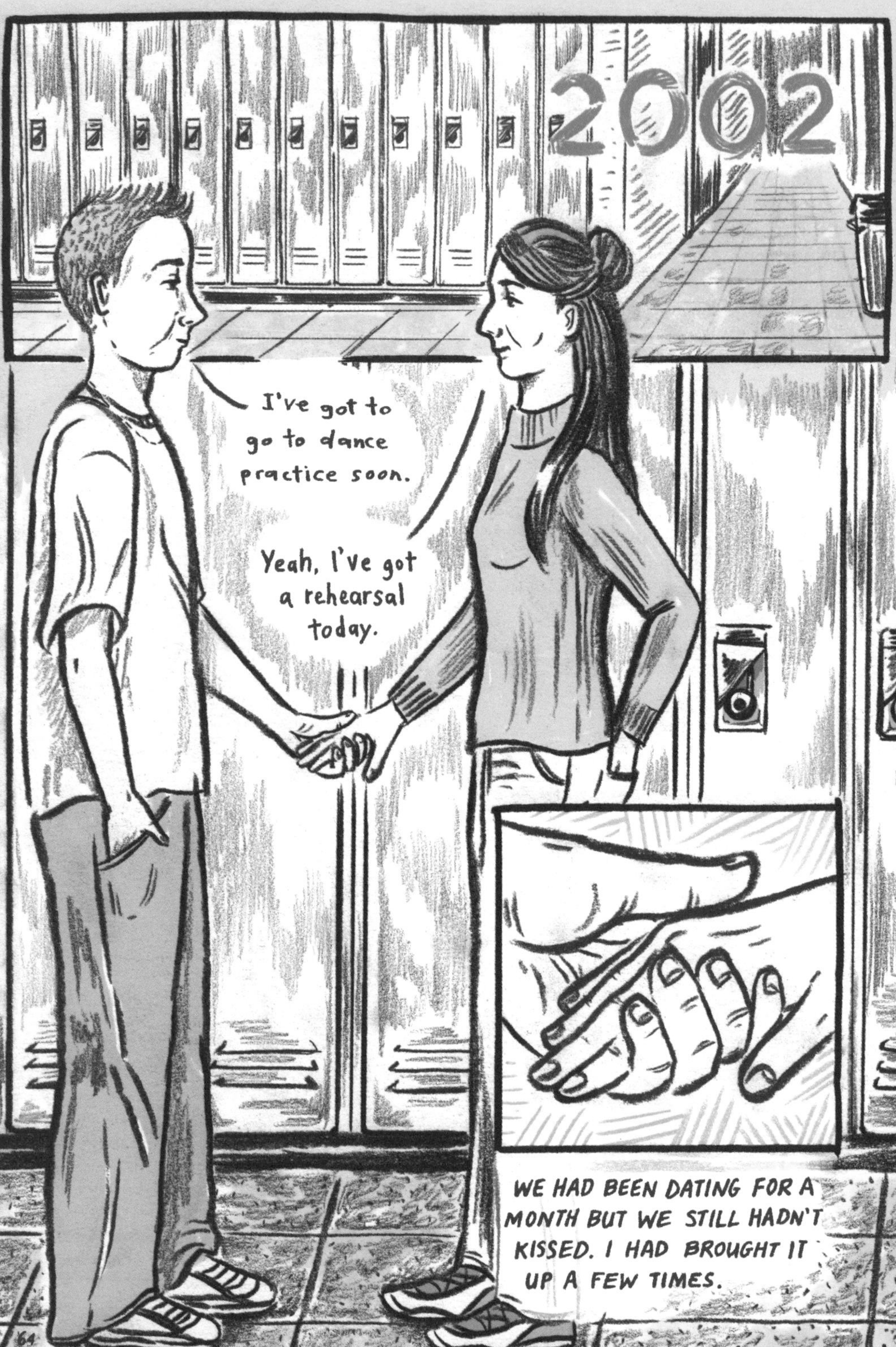
2002
I've got to go to dance practice soon.
Yeah, I've got a rehearsal today.
WE HAD BEEN DATING FOR A MONTH BUT WE STILL HADN'T KISSED. I HAD BROUGHT IT UP A FEW TIMES.

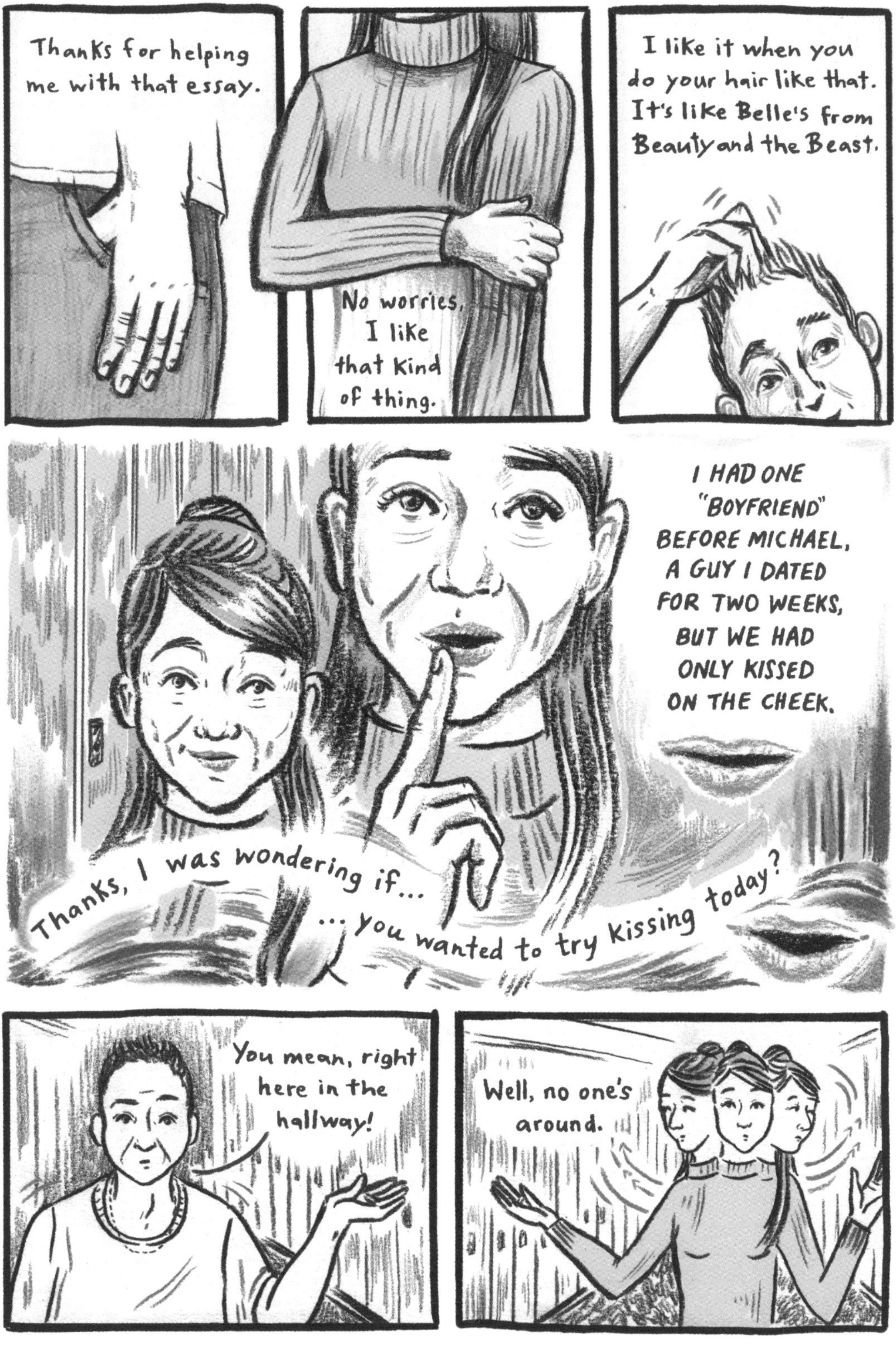
Thanks for helping me with that essay.
No worries, I like that kind of thing.
I like it when you do your hair like that. It's like Belle's from Beauty and the Beast.
I HAD ONE "BOYFRIEND" BEFORE MICHAEL, A GUY I DATED FOR TWO WEEKS, BUT WE HAD ONLY KISSED ON THE CHEEK.
Thanks, I was wondering if...
... you wanted to try kissing today?
You mean, right here in the hallway!
Well, no one's around.

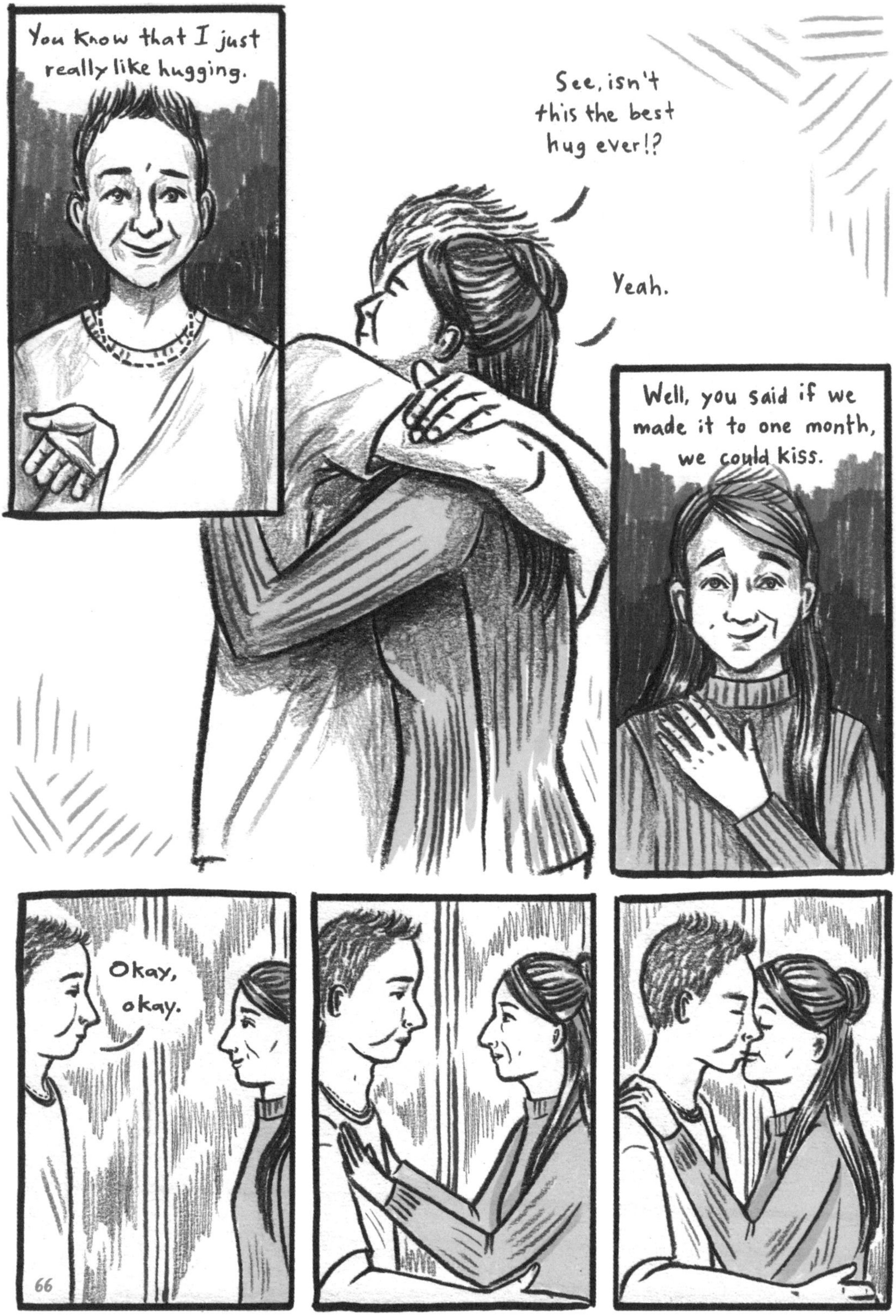
You know that I just really like hugging.
See, isn't this the best hug ever!?
Yeah.
Well, you said if we made it to one month, we could kiss.
Okay, okay.

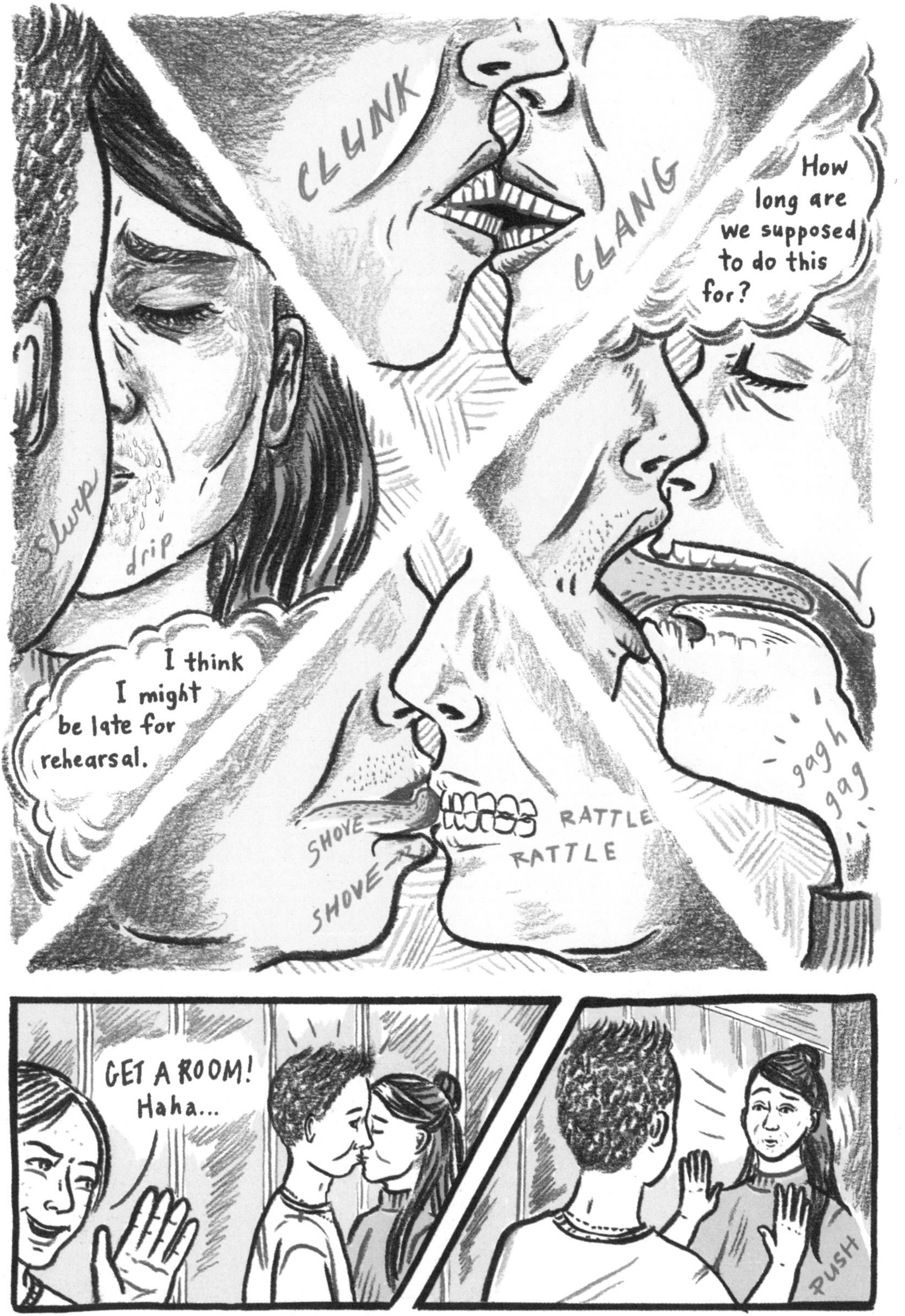
CLUNK
CLANG
How long are we supposed to do this for?
Slurp
drip
I think I might be late for rehearsal.
SHOVE
SHOVE
RATTLE
RATTLE
gagh
gag
GET A ROOM! Haha...
PUSH

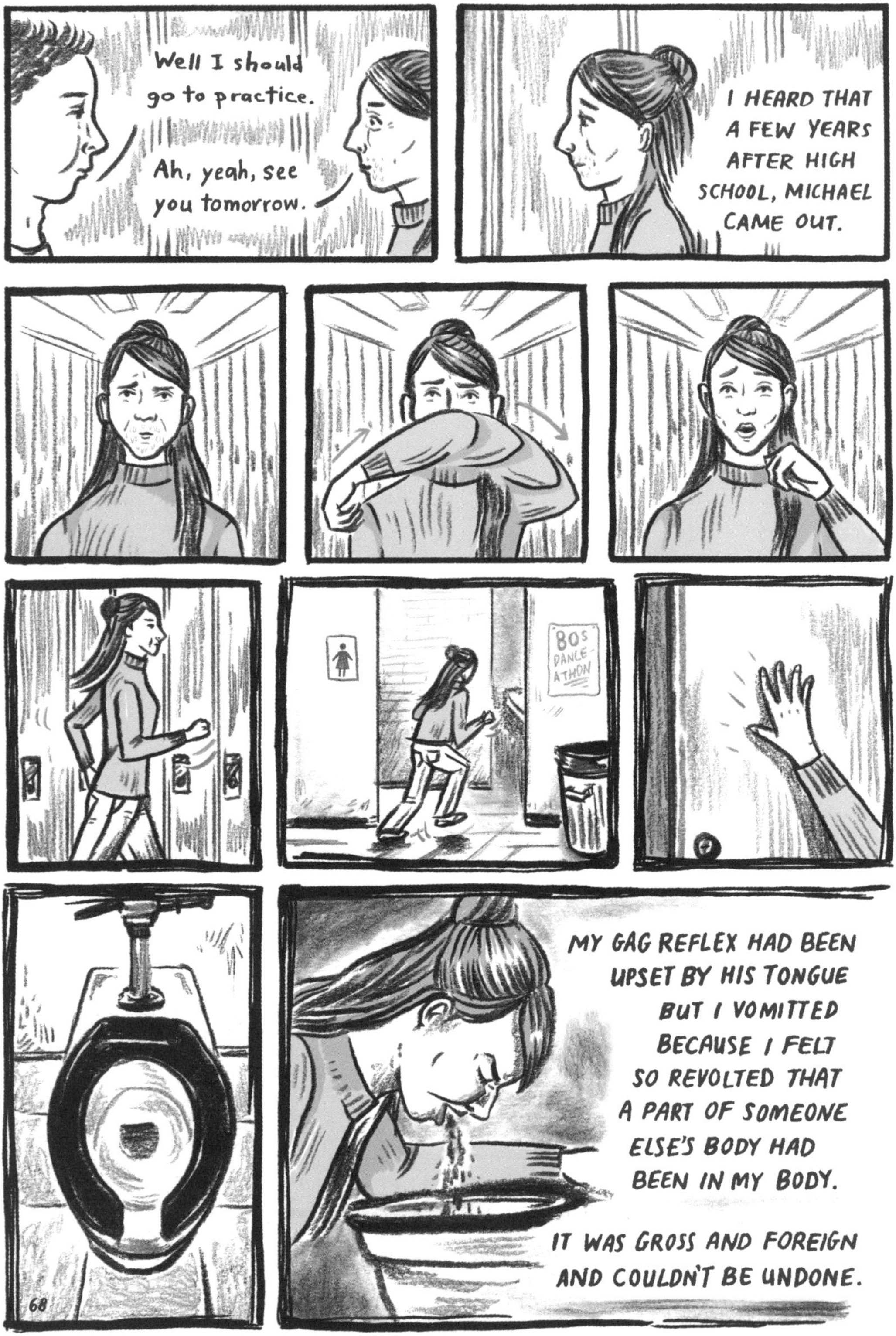
Well I should go to practice.
Ah, yeah, see you tomorrow.
I HEARD THAT A FEW YEARS AFTER HIGH SCHOOL, MICHAEL CAME OUT.
80s DANCE-ATHON
MY GAG REFLEX HAD BEEN UPSET BY HIS TONGUE BUT I VOMITTED BECAUSE I FELT SO REVOLTED THAT A PART OF SOMEONE ELSE'S BODY HAD BEEN IN MY BODY.
IT WAS GROSS AND FOREIGN AND COULDN'T BE UNDONE.

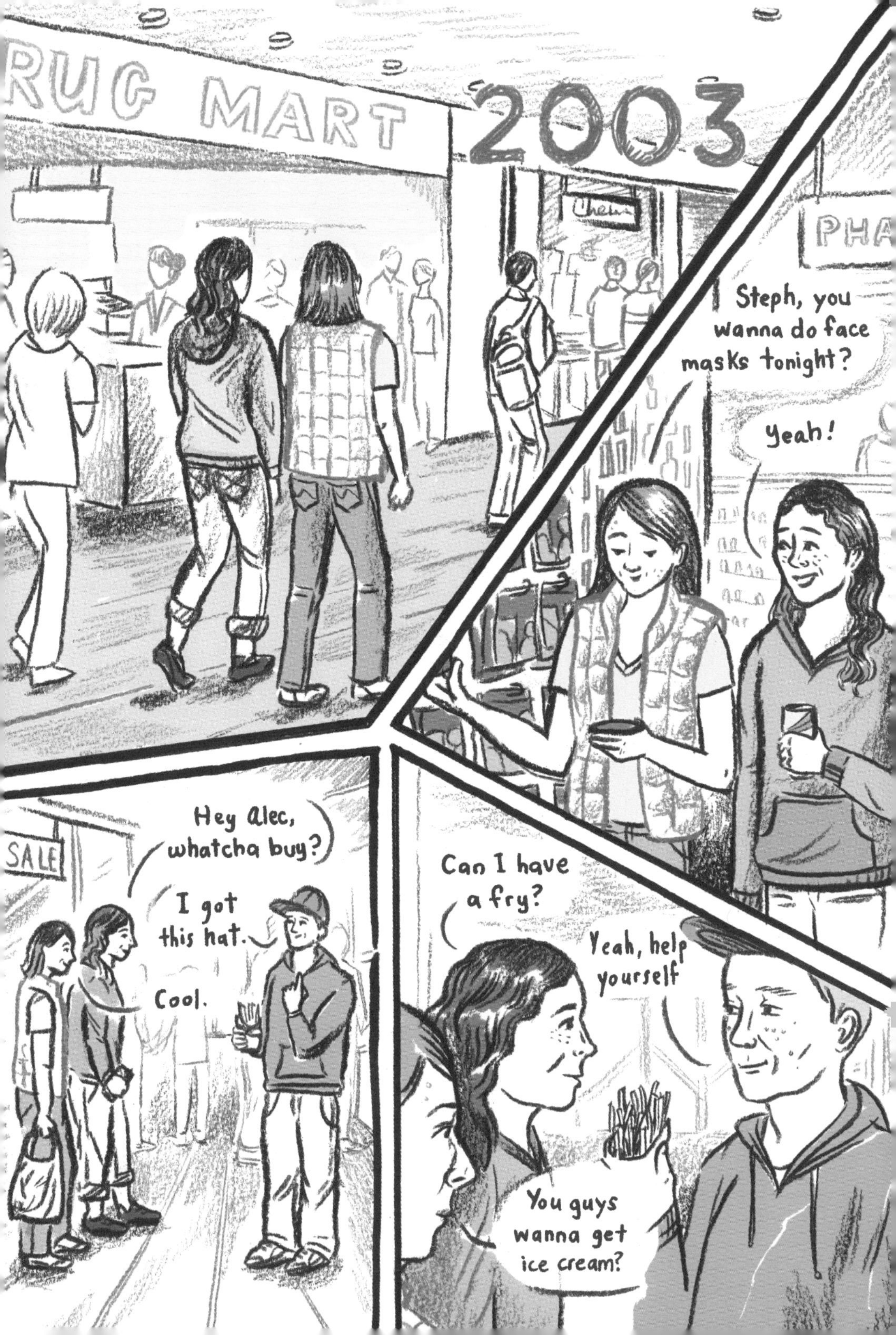
RUG MART
2003
PHA
Steph, you wanna do face masks tonight?
Yeah!
SALE
Hey alec, whatcha buy?
I got this hat.
Cool.
Can I have a fry?
Yeah, help yourself
You guys wanna get ice cream?

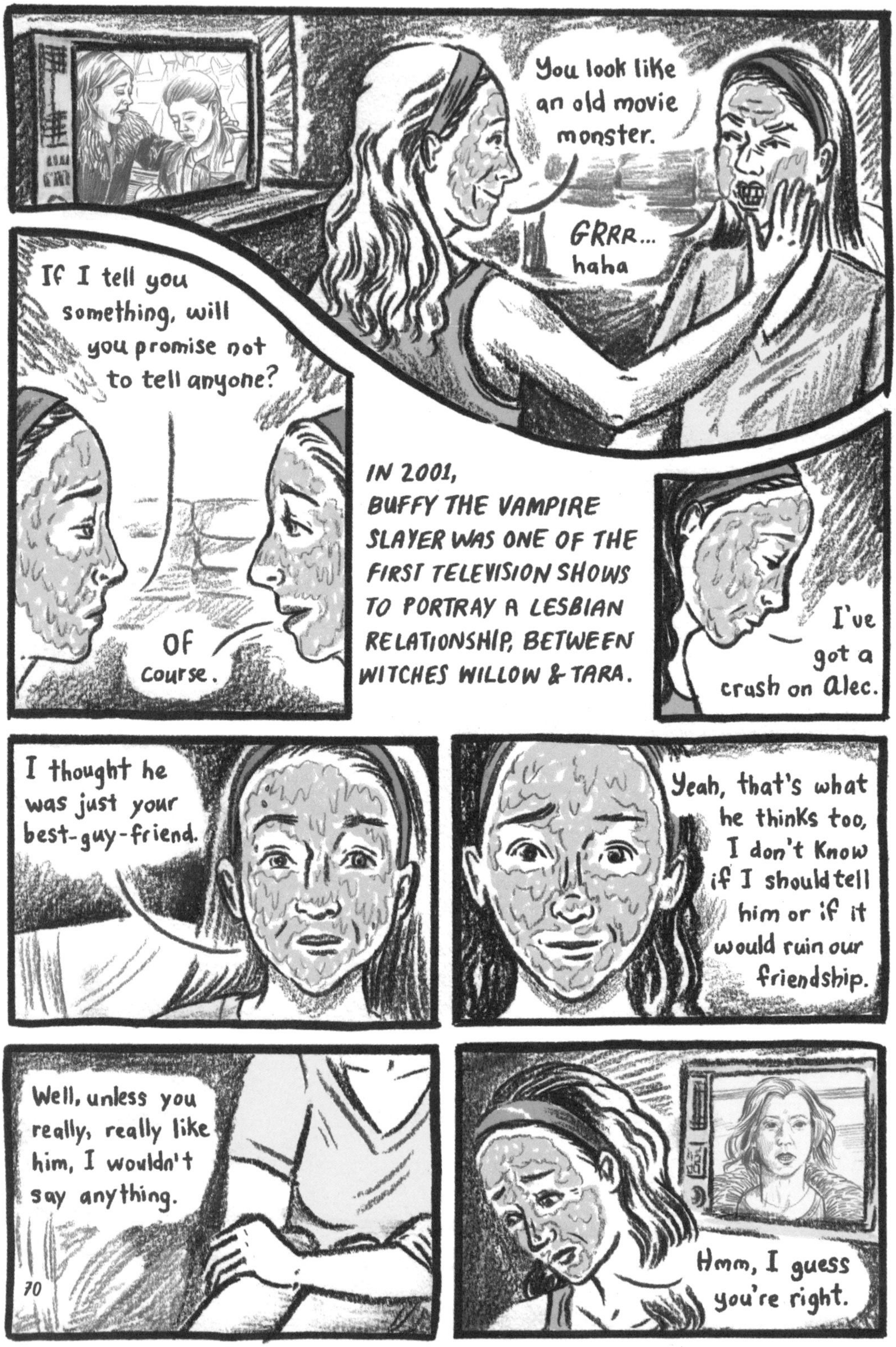
You look like an old movie monster.
GRRR... haha
If I tell you something, will you promise not to tell anyone?
Of course.
IN 2001, BUFFY THE VAMPIRE SLAYER WAS ONE OF THE FIRST TELEVISION SHOWS TO PORTRAY A LESBIAN RELATIONSHIP, BETWEEN WITCHES WILLOW & TARA.
I've got a crush on Alec.
I thought he was just your best-guy-friend.
Yeah, that's what he thinks too, I don't know if I should tell him or if it would ruin our friendship.
Well, unless you really, really like him, I wouldn't say anything.
Hmm, I guess you're right.

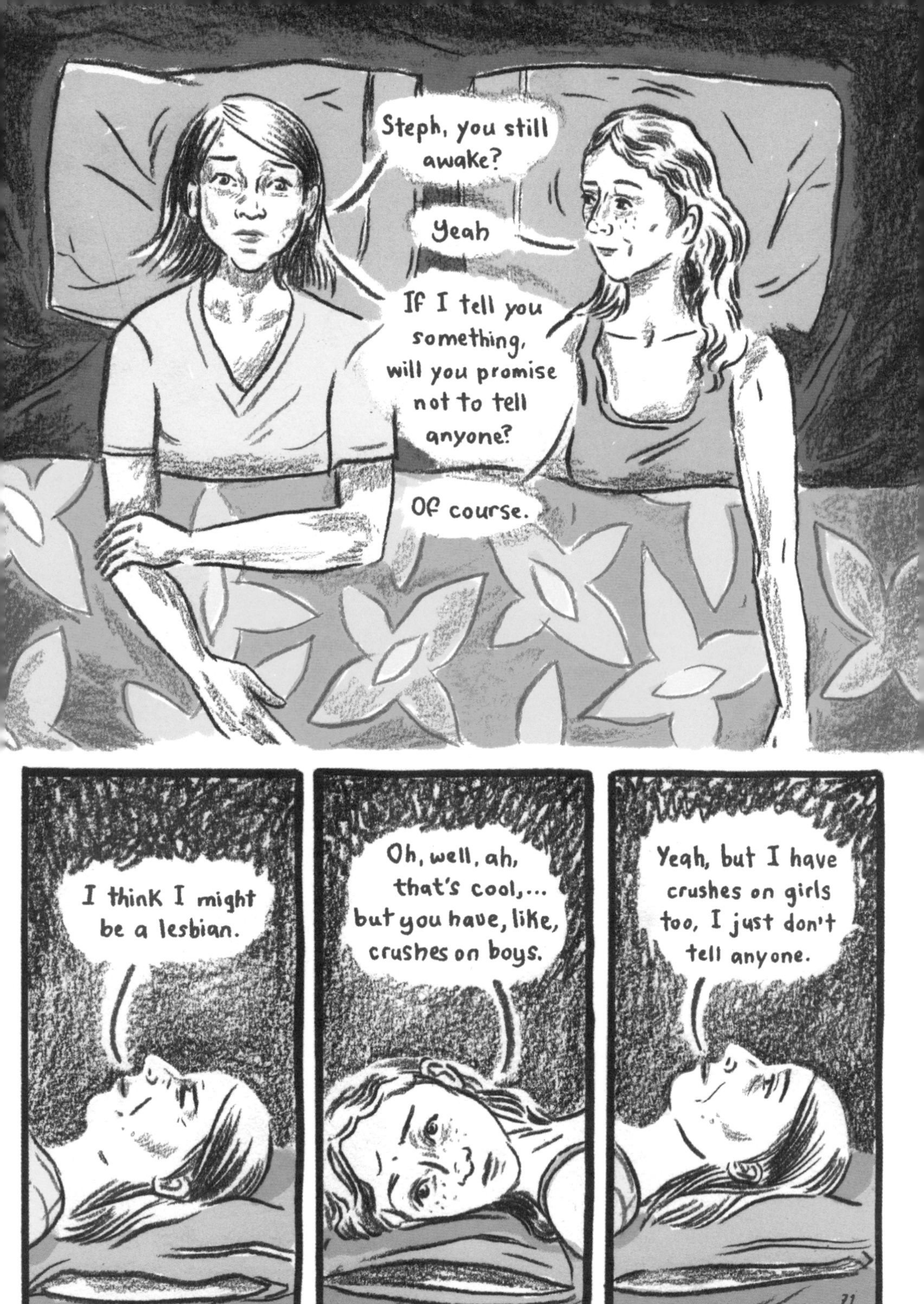
Steph, you still awake?
Yeah
If I tell you something, will you promise not to tell anyone?
Of course.
I think I might be a lesbian.
Oh, well, ah, that's cool,... but you have, like, crushes on boys.
Yeah, but I have crushes on girls too, I just don't tell anyone.

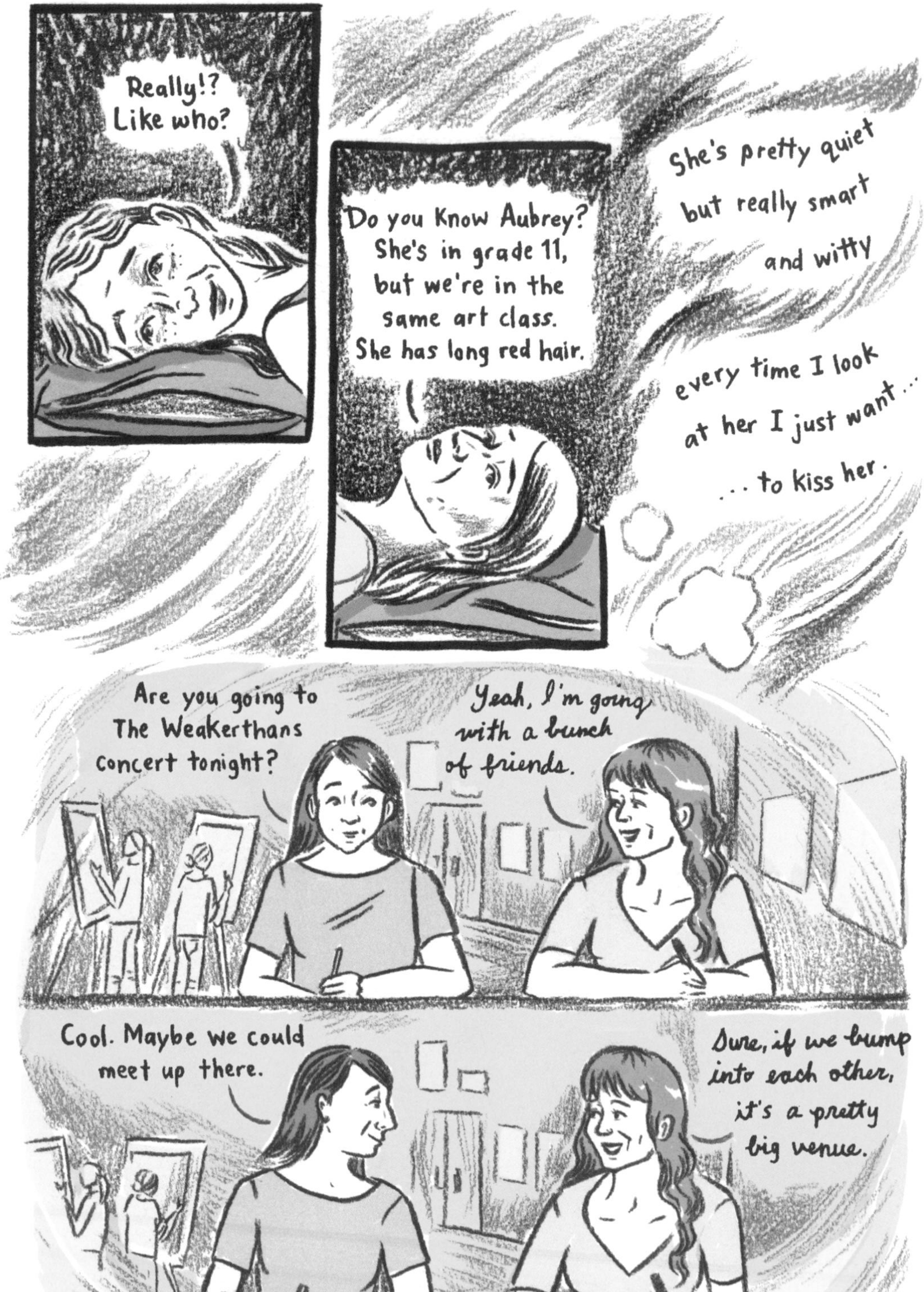

Really!? Like who?
Do you know Aubrey? She's in grade 11, but we're in the same art class. She has long red hair.
She's pretty quiet
but really smart
and witty
every time I look at her I just want...
... to kiss her.
Are you going to The Weakerthans concert tonight?
Yeah, I'm going with a bunch of friends.
Cool. Maybe we could meet up there.
Sure, if we bump into each other, it's a pretty big venue.

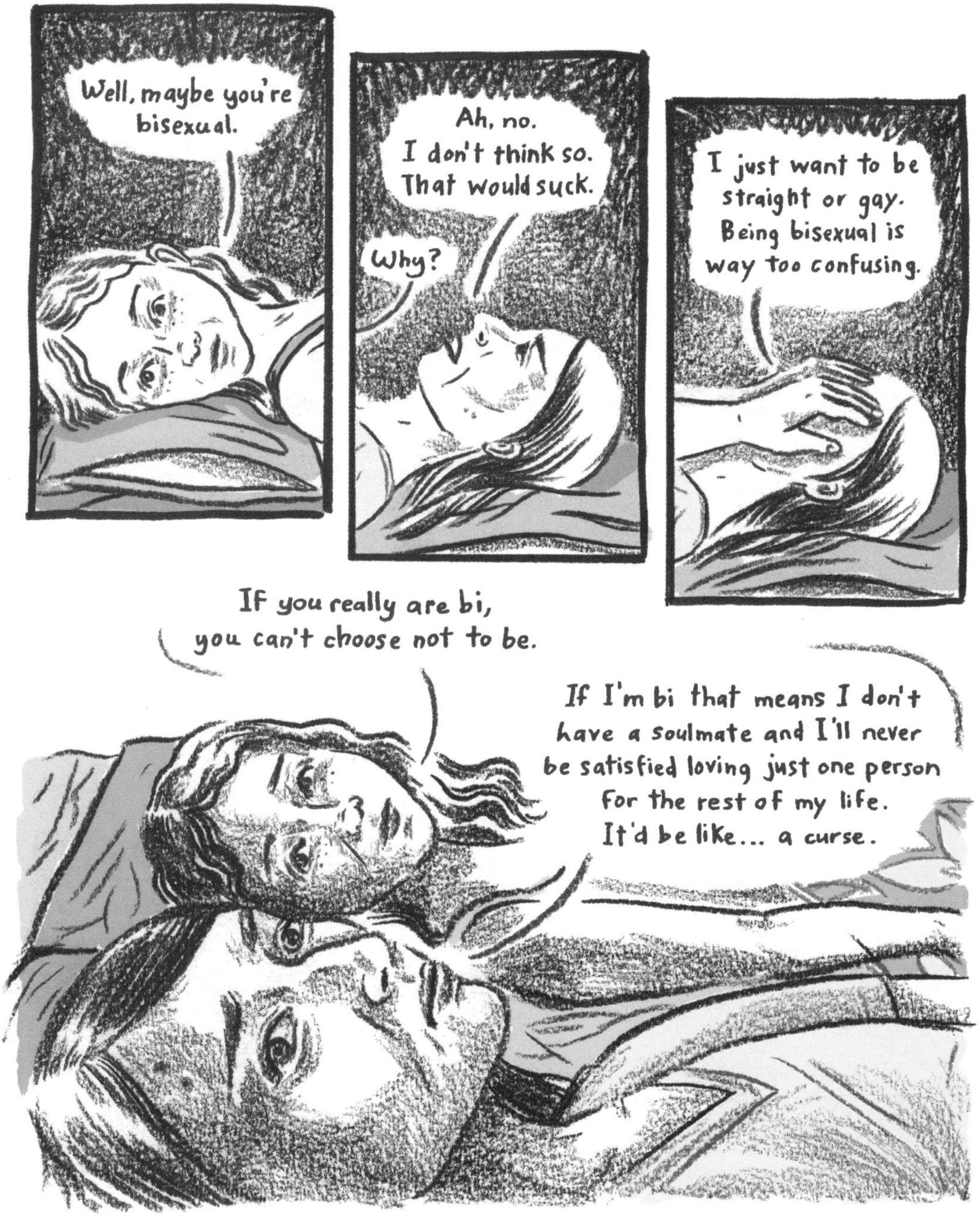
Well, maybe you're bisexual.
Ah, no. I don't think so. That would suck.
Why?
I just want to be straight or gay. Being bisexual is way too confusing.
If you really are bi, you can't choose not to be.
If I'm bi that means I don't have a soulmate and I'll never be satisfied loving just one person for the rest of my life. It'd be like... a curse.

WILLOW'S NEW IDENTITY AS A LESBIAN WAS POSITIVELY RECEIVED BY VIEWERS BUT THE NEW LABEL IGNORED THE TWO YEAR RELATIONSHIP SHE'D HAD WITH OZ, A MAN (AND WEREWOLF). NO ONE WAS CALLING WILLOW BISEXUAL. THERE WEREN'T ANY BISEXUALS ON TV.

I DIDN'T KNOW ANY ADULTS WHO WERE OUT AND OPEN AS BISEXUALS EITHER.

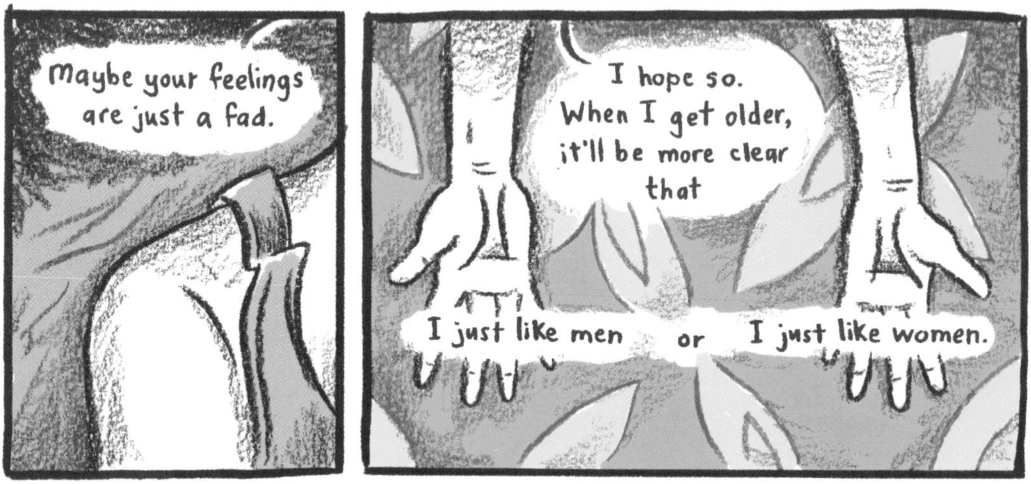
Maybe your feelings are just a fad.
I hope so. When I get older, it'll be more clear that
I just like men
or
I just like women.

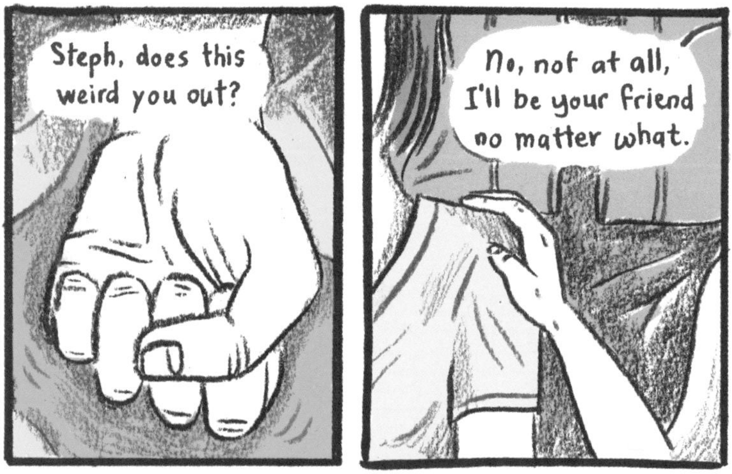
Steph, does this weird you out?
No, not at all, I'll be your friend no matter what.

OVER THE NEXT FEW MONTHS I DRIFTED AWAY FROM STEPH.

SHE HAD BEEN A GREAT FRIEND BUT I DIDN'T FEEL LIKE I FIT WITH HER CROWD.

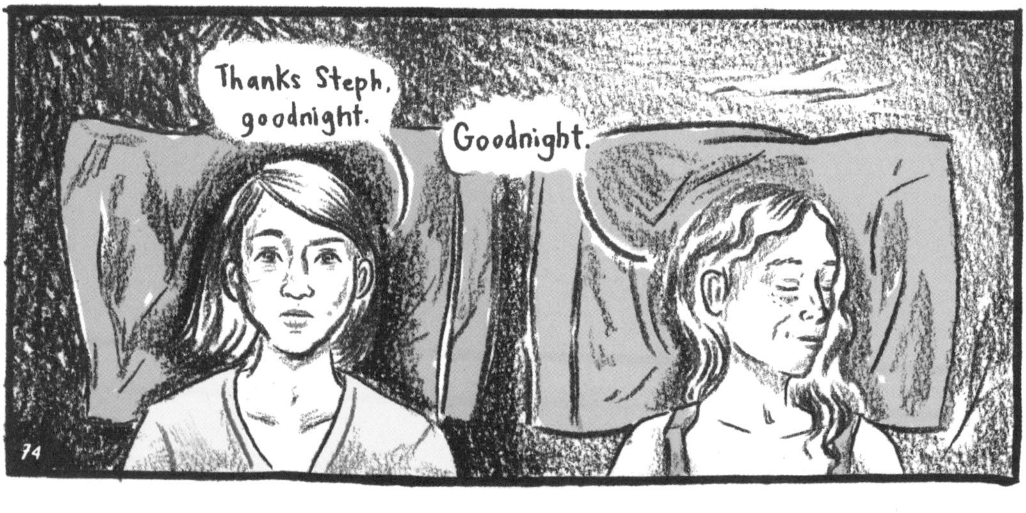
Thanks Steph, goodnight.
Goodnight.

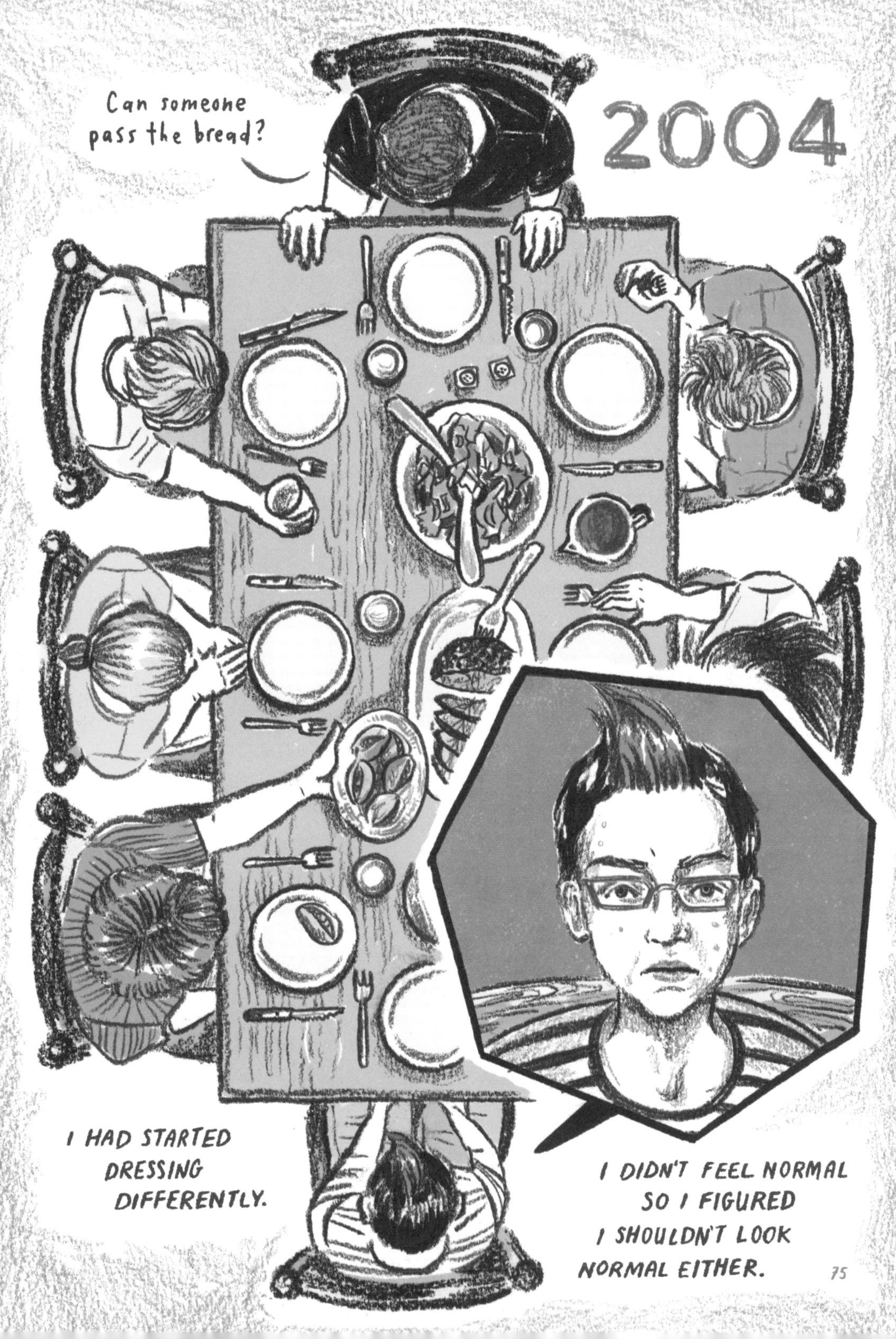
Can someone pass the bread?
2004
I HAD STARTED DRESSING DIFFERENTLY.
I DIDN'T FEEL NORMAL SO I FIGURED I SHOULDN'T LOOK NORMAL EITHER.

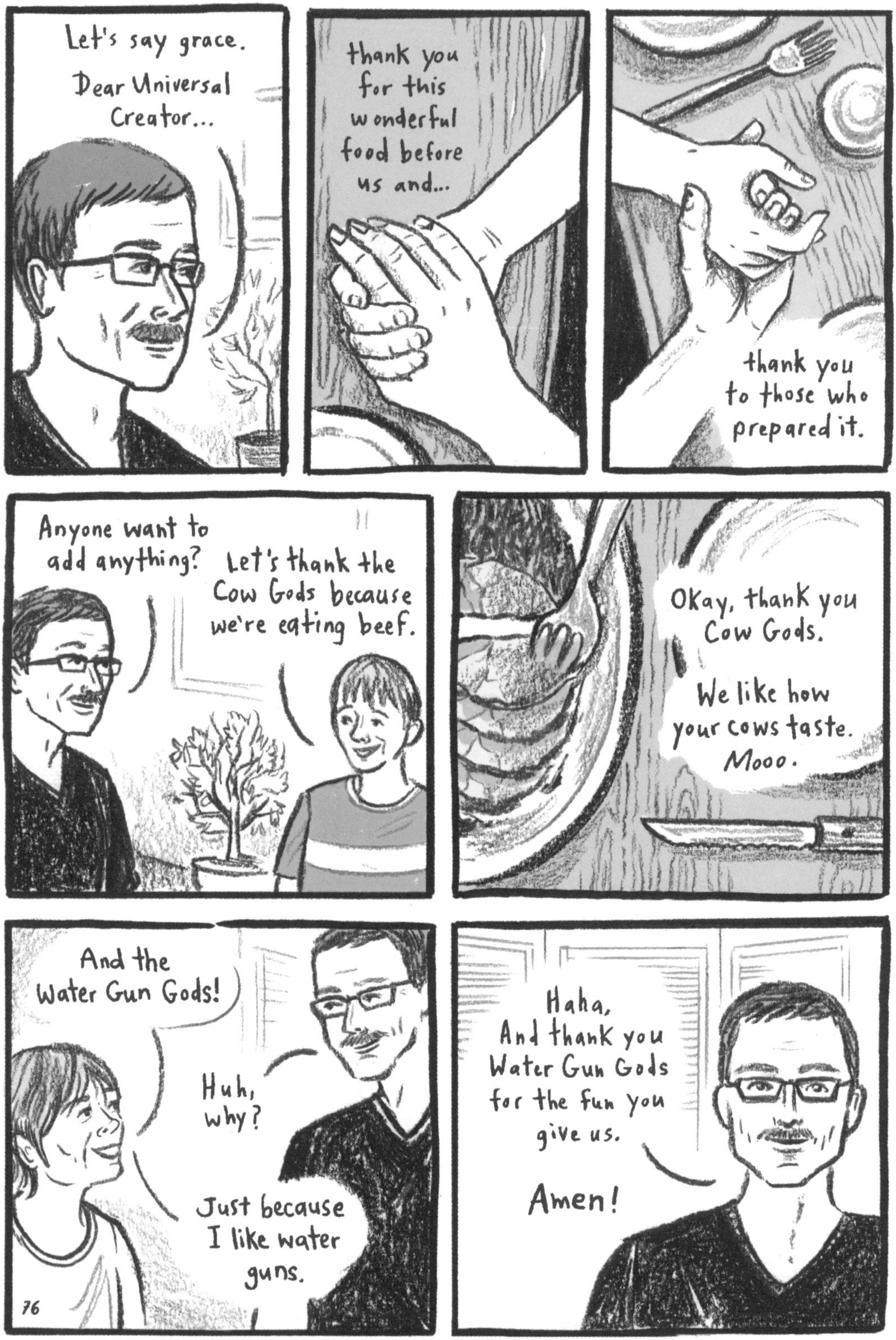
Let's say grace.
Dear Universal Creator...
thank you for this wonderful food before us and...
thank you to those who prepared it.
Anyone want to add anything?
Let's thank the Cow Gods because we're eating beef.
Okay, thank you Cow Gods.
We like how your cows taste. Mooo.
And the Water Gun Gods!
Huh, why?
Just because I like water guns.
Haha, And thank you Water Gun Gods for the fun you give us.
Amen!

I DYED MY HAIR AND CUT IT MYSELF WHENEVER I FELT THE URGE, USUALLY AFTER A BREAK-UP FROM A SHORT RELATIONSHIP WITH A BOY.

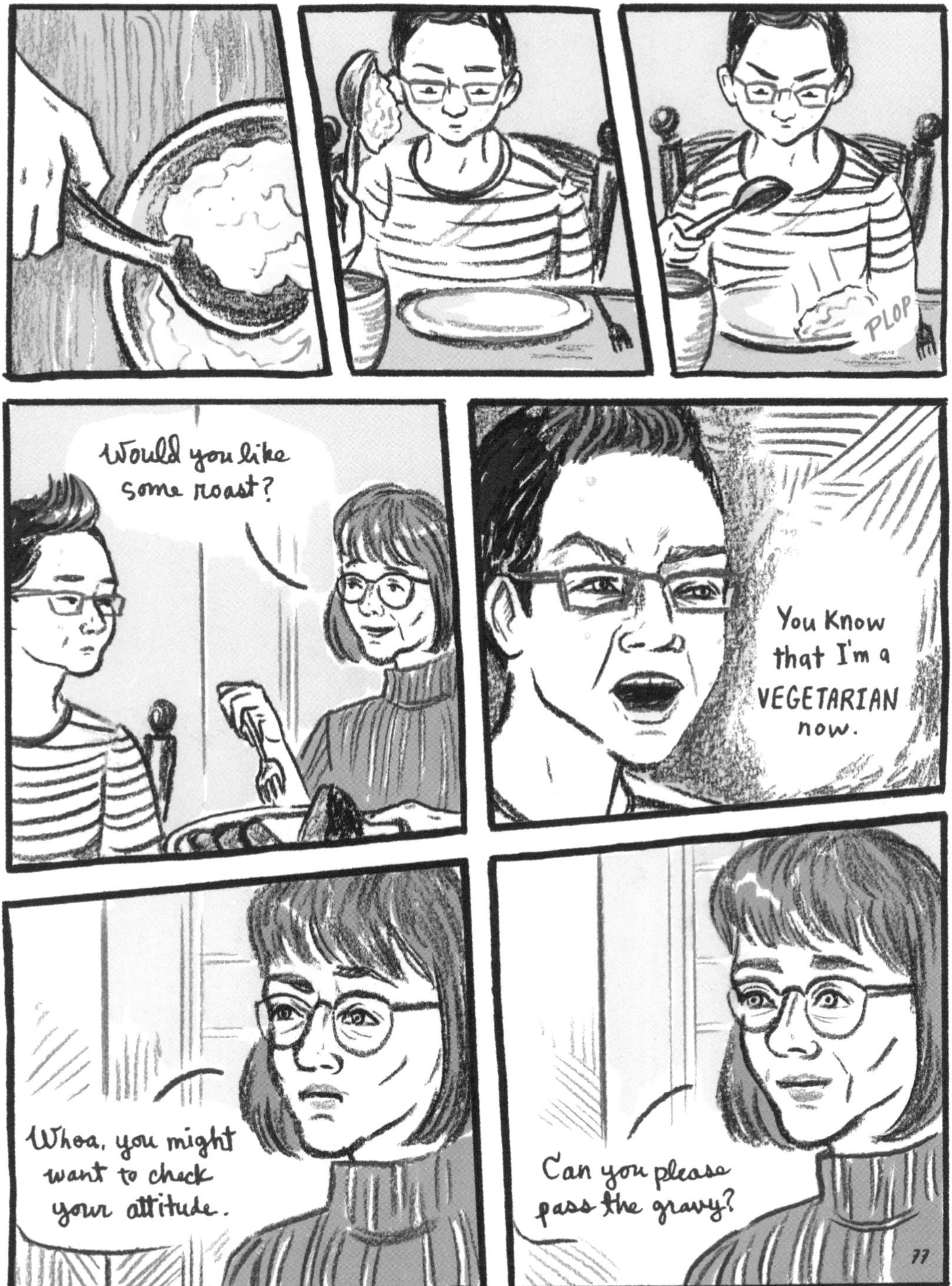
PLOP
Would you like some roast?
You know that I'm a VEGETARIAN now.
Whoa, you might want to check your attitude.
Can you please pass the gravy?

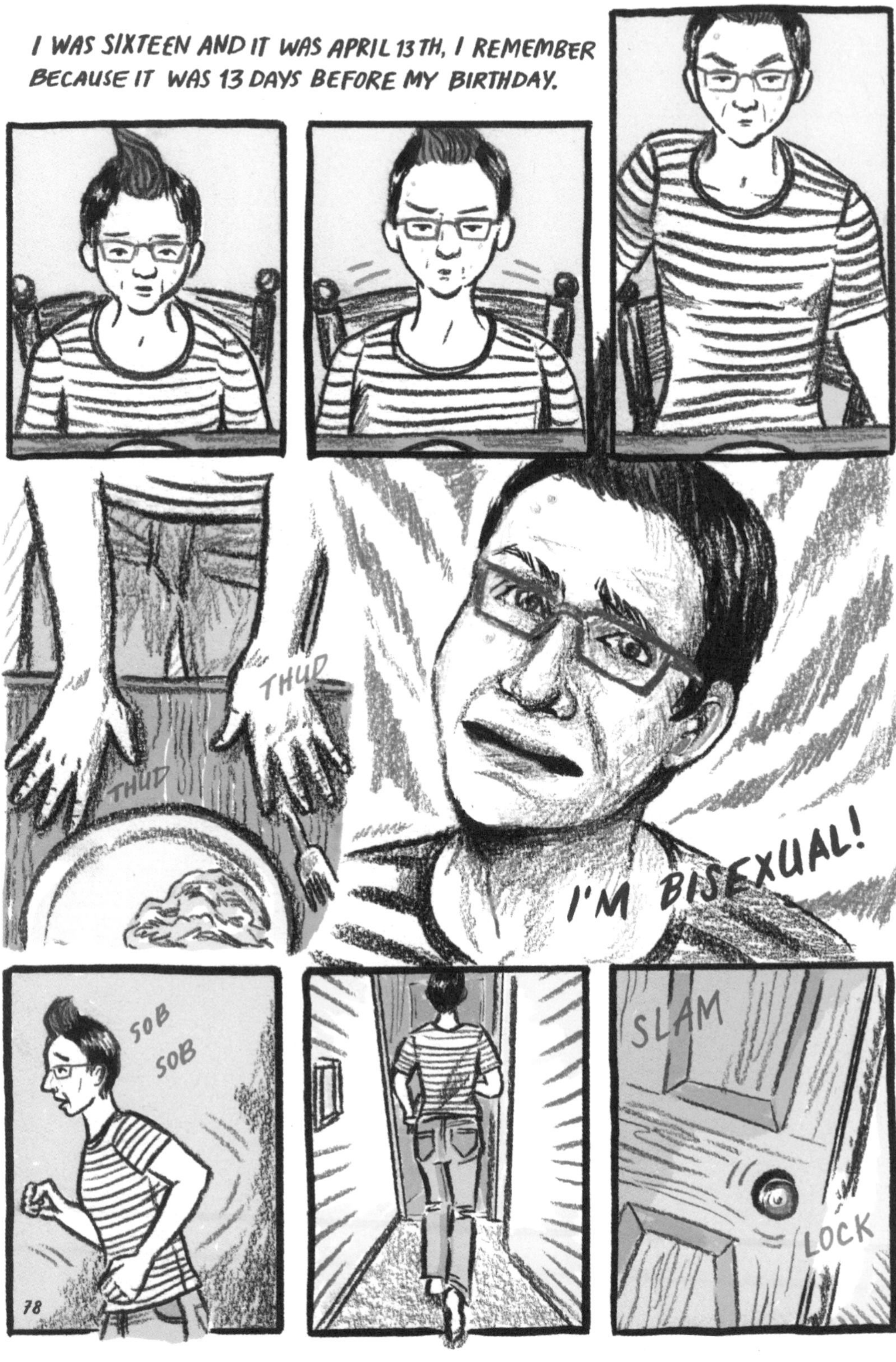
I WAS SIXTEEN AND IT WAS APRIL 13TH, I REMEMBER BECAUSE IT WAS 13 DAYS BEFORE MY BIRTHDAY.
THUD
THUD
I'M BISEXUAL!
SOB
SOB
SLAM
LOCK

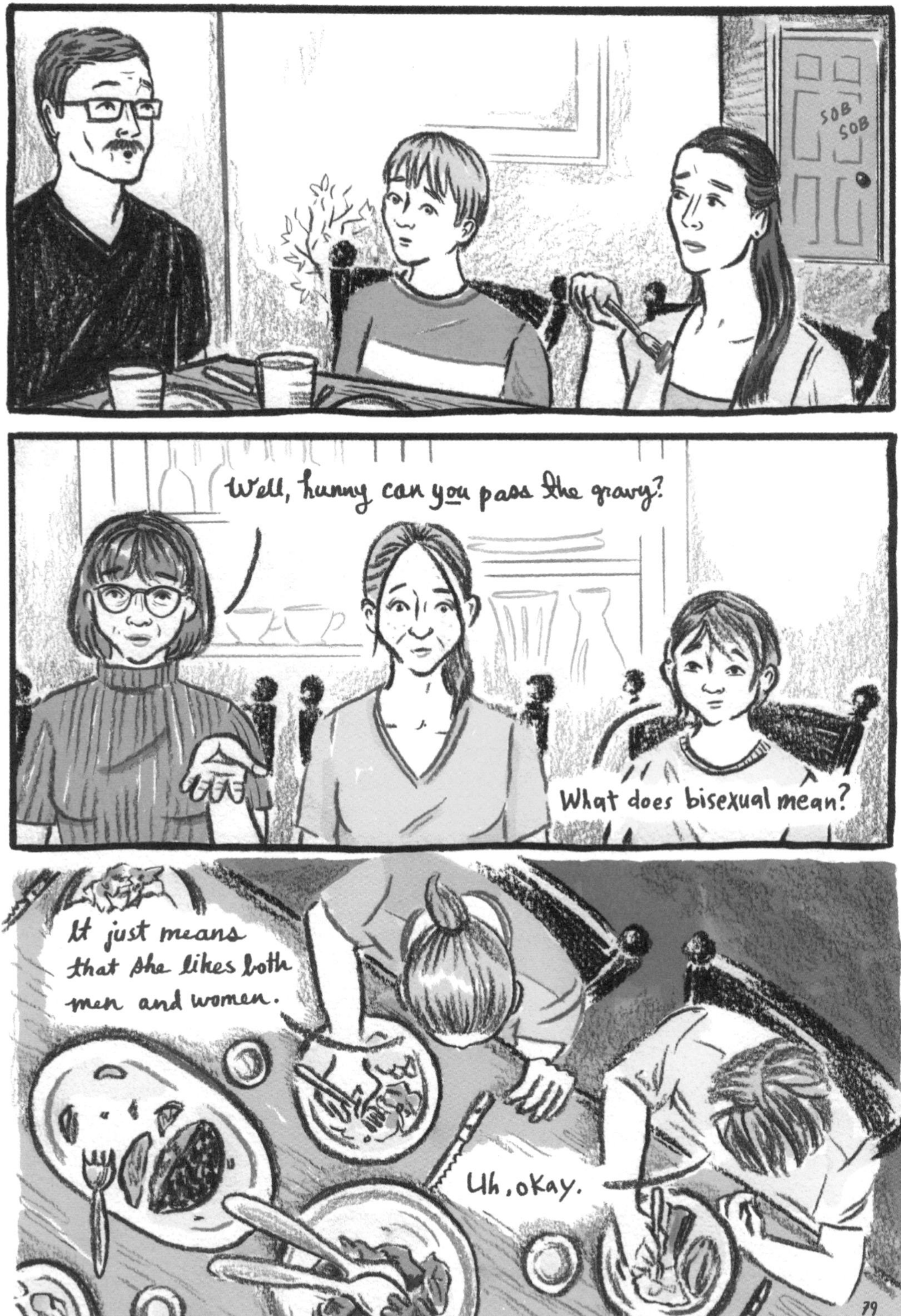
SOB SOB
Well, hunny can you pass the gravy?
What does bisexual mean?
It just means that she likes both men and women.
Uh, okay.

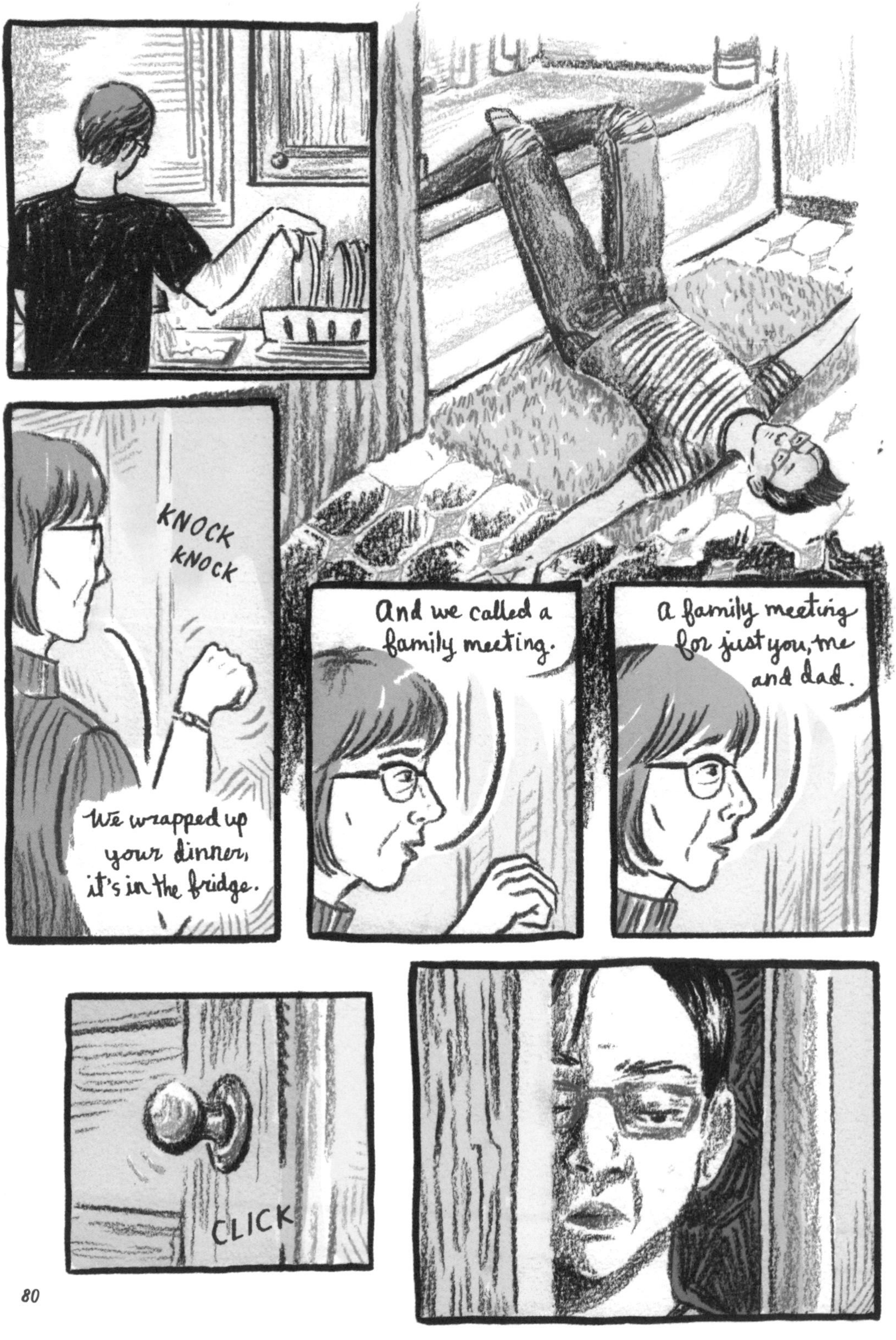

KNOCK KNOCK
We wrapped up your dinner, it's in the fridge.
And we called a family meeting.
A family meeting for just you, me and dad.
CLICK

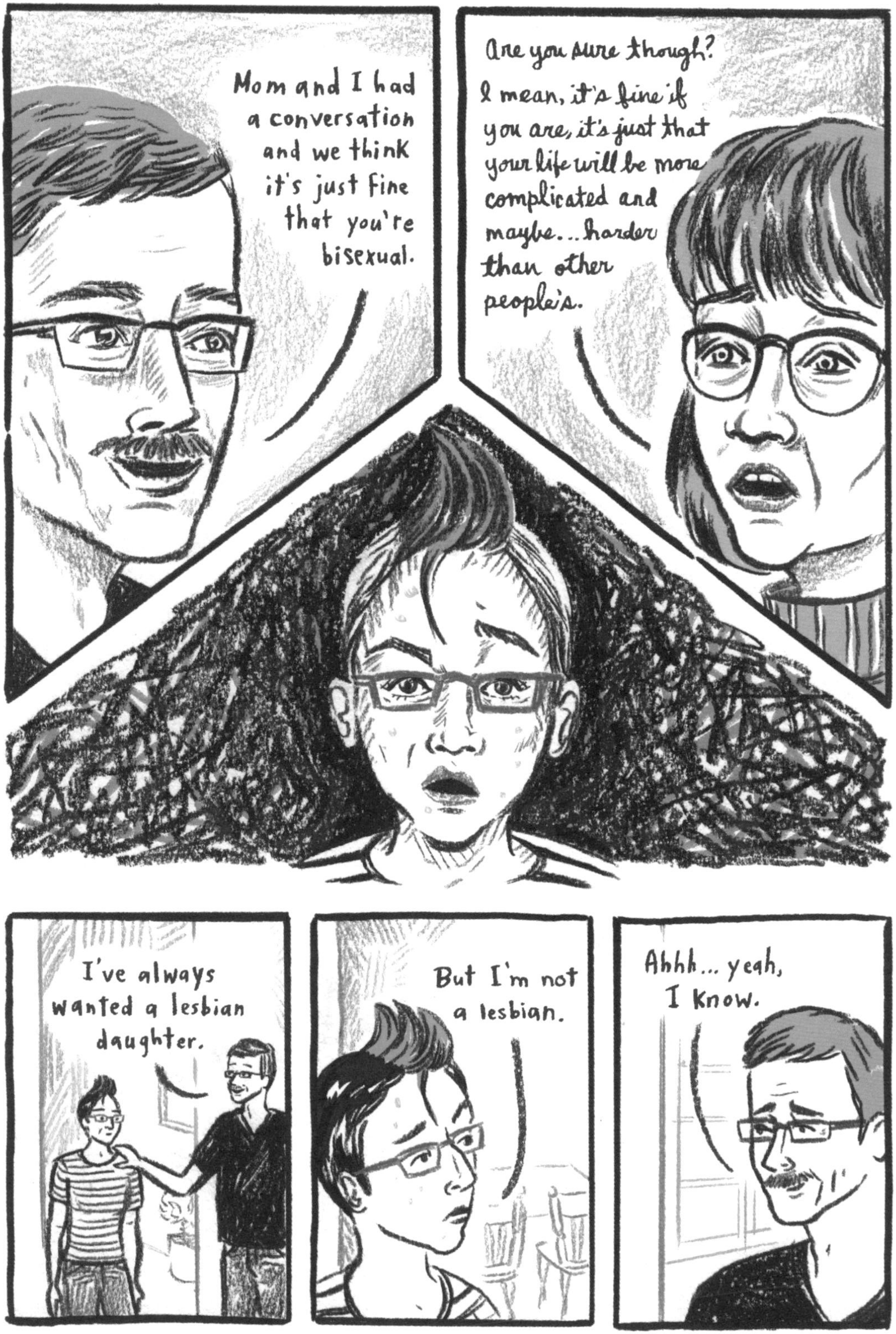
Mom and I had a conversation and we think it's just fine that you're bisexual.
Are you sure though?
I mean, it's fine if you are, it's just that your life will be more complicated and maybe... harder than other people's.
I've always wanted a lesbian daughter.
But I'm not a lesbian.
Ahhh... yeah, I know.

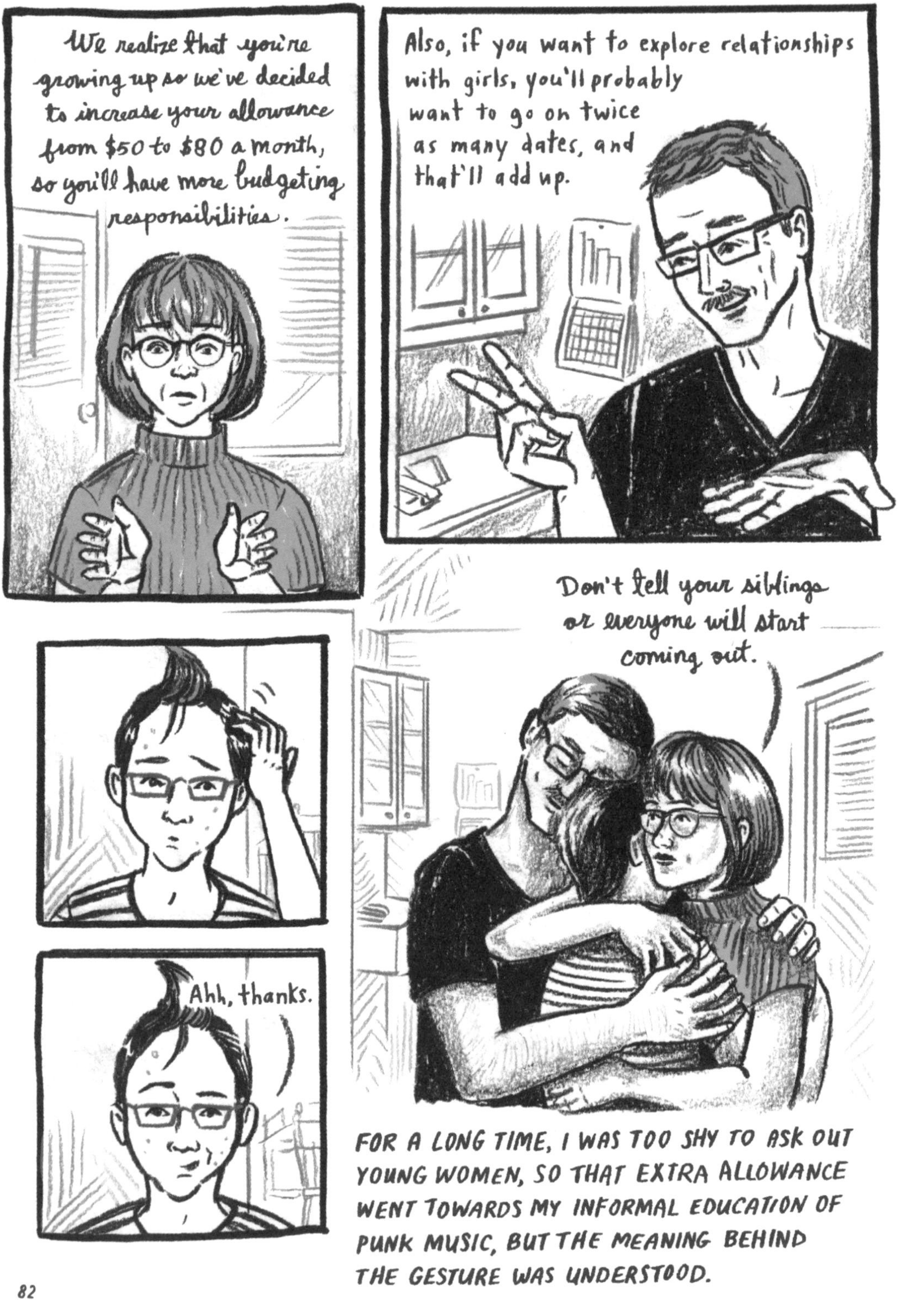
We realize that you're growing up so we've decided to increase your allowance from $50 to $80 a month, so you'll have more budgeting responsibilities.
Also, if you want to explore relationships with girls, you'll probably want to go on twice as many dates, and that'll add up.
Ahh, thanks.
Don't tell your siblings or everyone will start coming out.
FOR A LONG TIME, I WAS TOO SHY TO ASK OUT YOUNG WOMEN, SO THAT EXTRA ALLOWANCE WENT TOWARDS MY INFORMAL EDUCATION OF PUNK MUSIC, BUT THE MEANING BEHIND THE GESTURE WAS UNDERSTOOD.

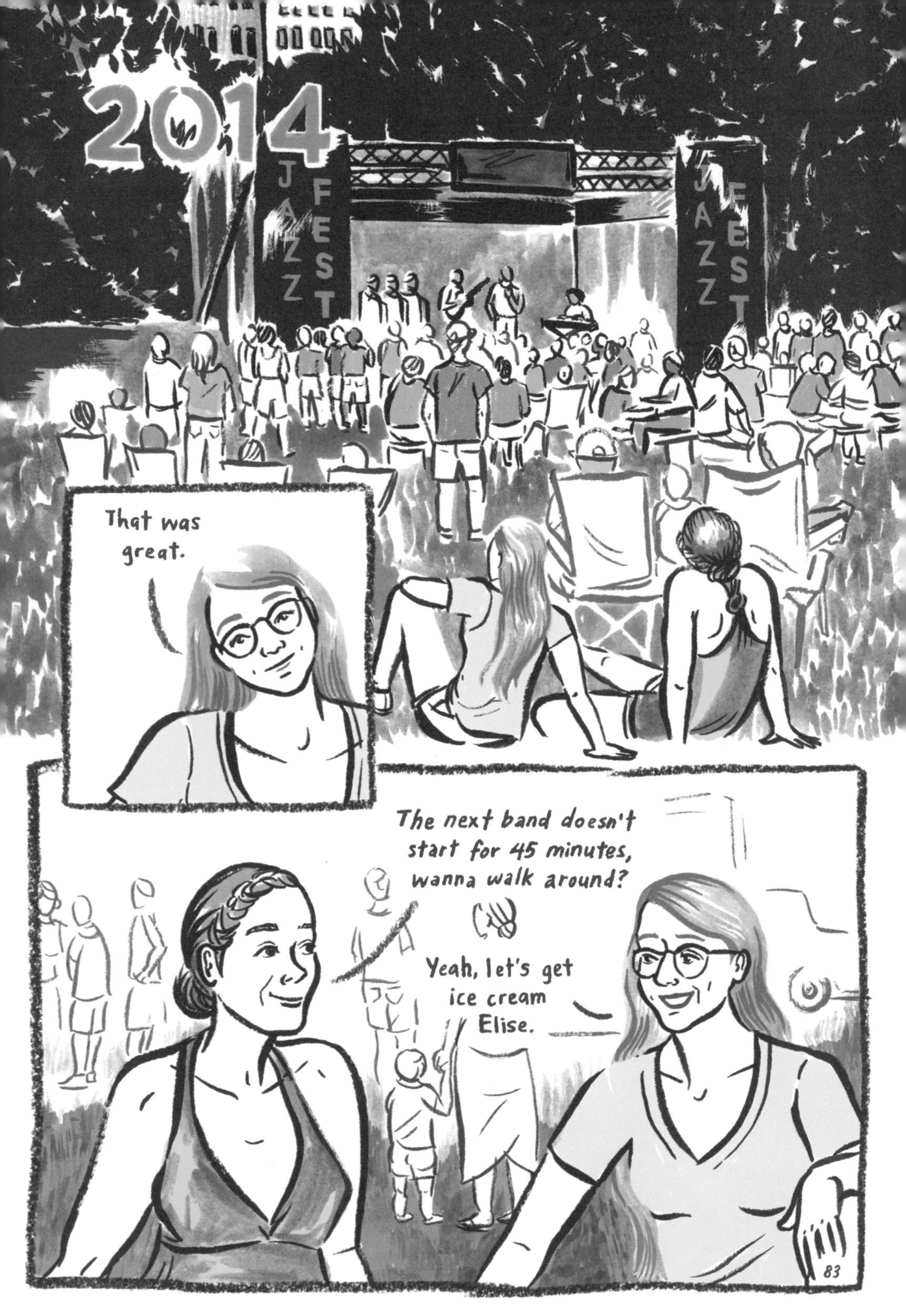
2014
JAZZ FEST
JAZZ FEST
That was great.
The next band doesn't start for 45 minutes, wanna walk around?
Yeah, let's get ice cream Elise.

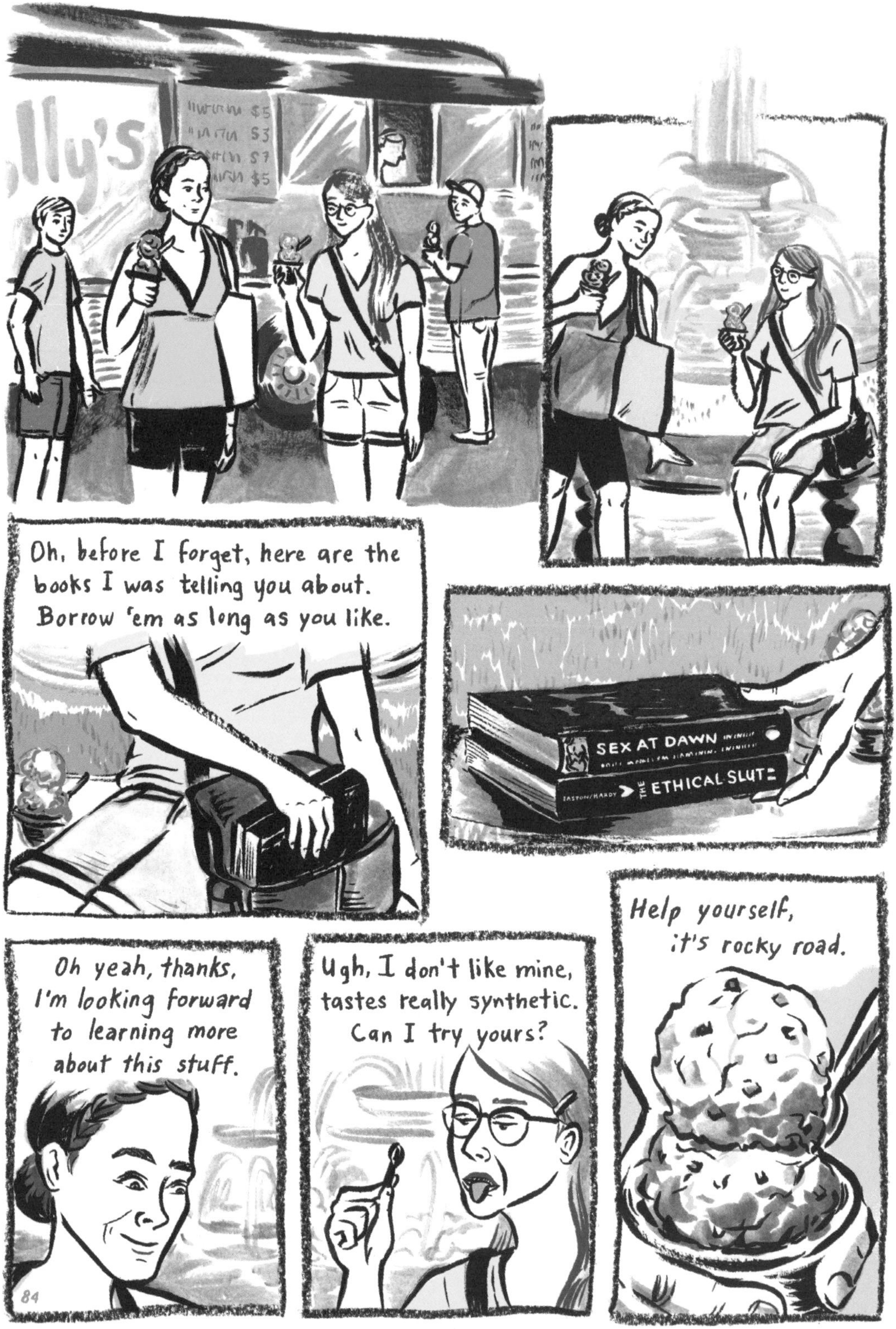
lly's
$5
$3
$7
$5
Oh, before I forget, here are the books I was telling you about. Borrow 'em as long as you like.
SEX AT DAWN
THE ETHICAL SLUT
EASTON/HARDY
Oh yeah, thanks, I'm looking forward to learning more about this stuff.
Ugh, I don't like mine, tastes really synthetic. Can I try yours?
Help yourself, it's rocky road.

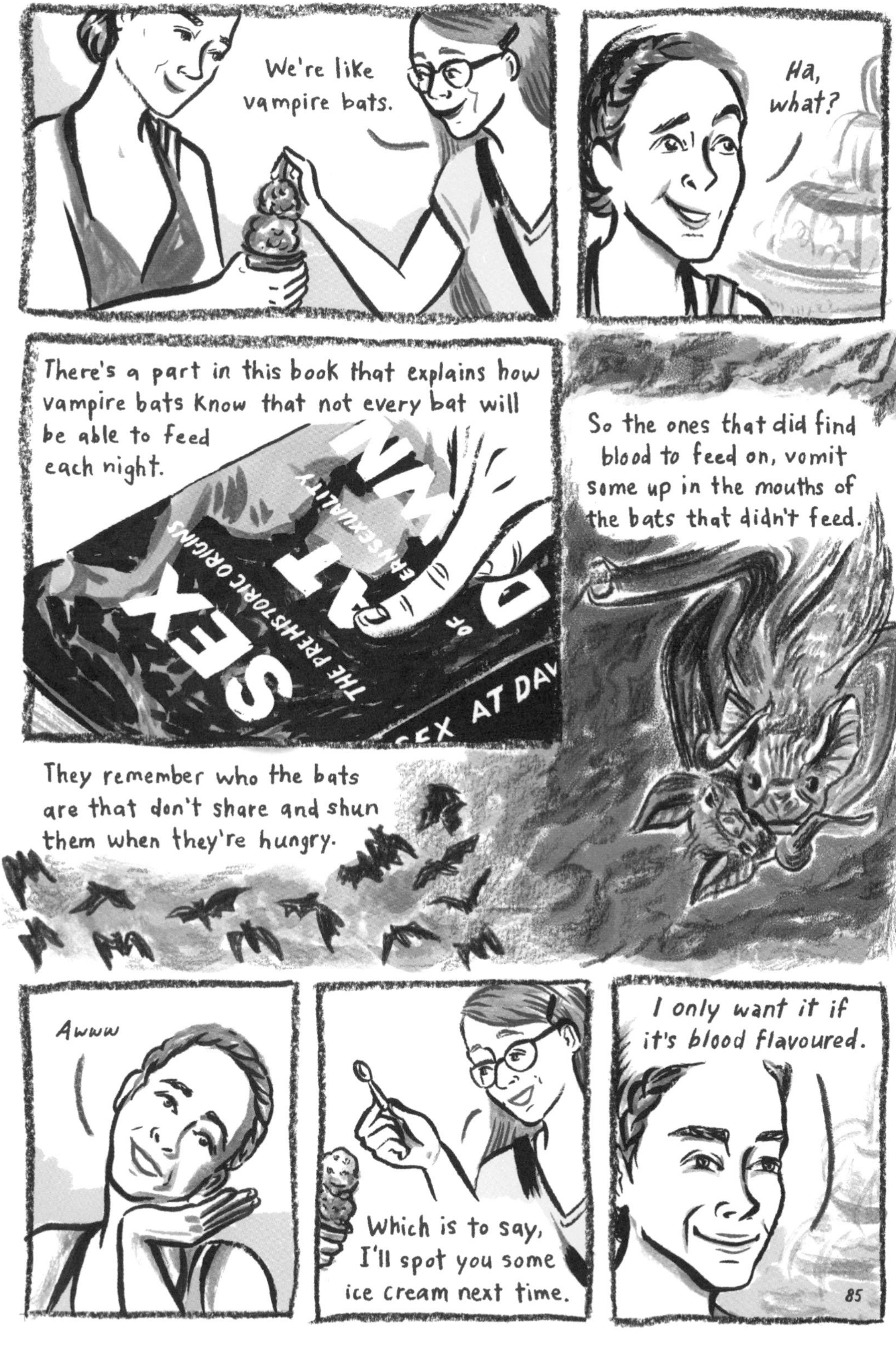
We're like vampire bats.
Ha, what?
There's a part in this book that explains how vampire bats know that not every bat will be able to feed each night.
SEX AT DAWN
THE PREHISTORIC ORIGINS OF MODERN SEXUALITY
SEX AT DAV
So the ones that did find blood to feed on, vomit some up in the mouths of the bats that didn't feed.
They remember who the bats are that don't share and shun them when they're hungry.
Awww
Which is to say, I'll spot you some ice cream next time.
I only want it if it's blood flavoured.

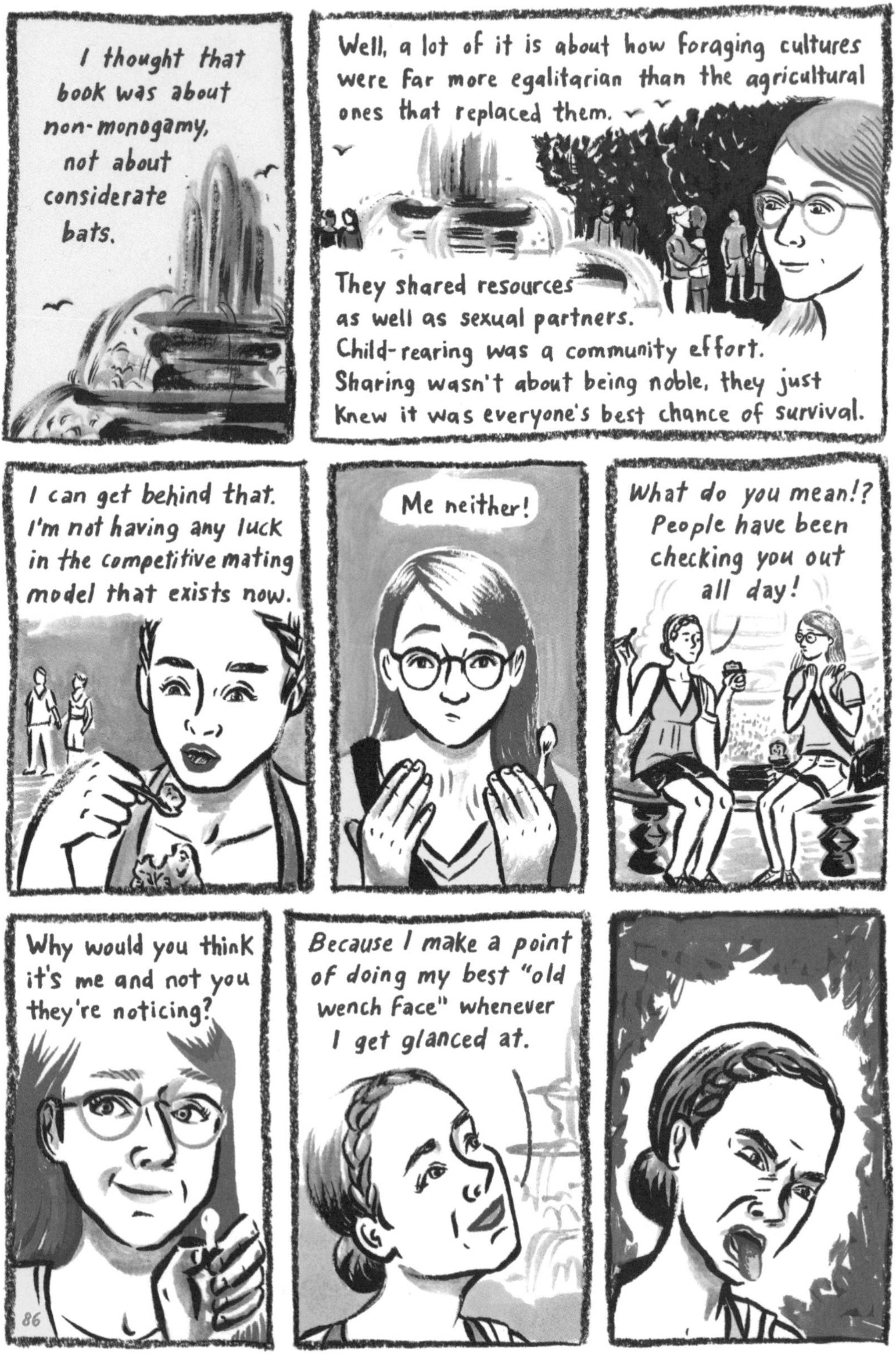
I thought that book was about non-monogamy, not about considerate bats.
Well, a lot of it is about how foraging cultures were far more egalitarian than the agricultural ones that replaced them.
They shared resources as well as sexual partners. Child-rearing was a community effort. Sharing wasn't about being noble, they just knew it was everyone's best chance of survival.
I can get behind that. I'm not having any luck in the competitive mating model that exists now.
Me neither!
What do you mean!? People have been checking you out all day!
Why would you think it's me and not you they're noticing?
Because I make a point of doing my best "old wench face" whenever I get glanced at.

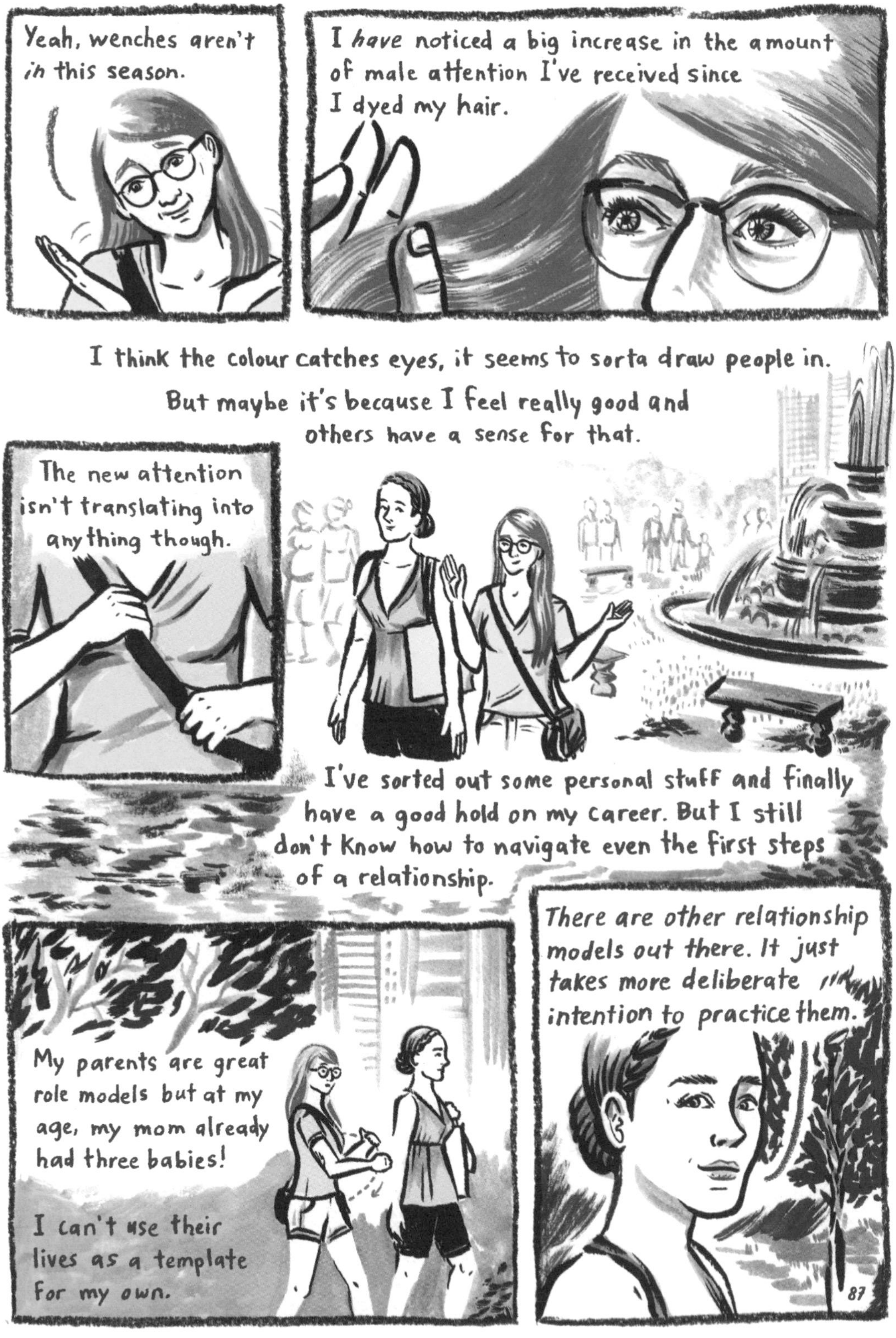
Yeah, wenches aren't *in* this season.
I *have* noticed a big increase in the amount of male attention I've received since I dyed my hair.
I think the colour catches eyes, it seems to sorta draw people in.
But maybe it's because I feel really good and others have a sense for that.
The new attention isn't translating into anything though.
I've sorted out some personal stuff and finally have a good hold on my career. But I still don't know how to navigate even the first steps of a relationship.
My parents are great role models but at my age, my mom already had three babies!
I can't use their lives as a template for my own.
There are other relationship models out there. It just takes more deliberate intention to practice them.

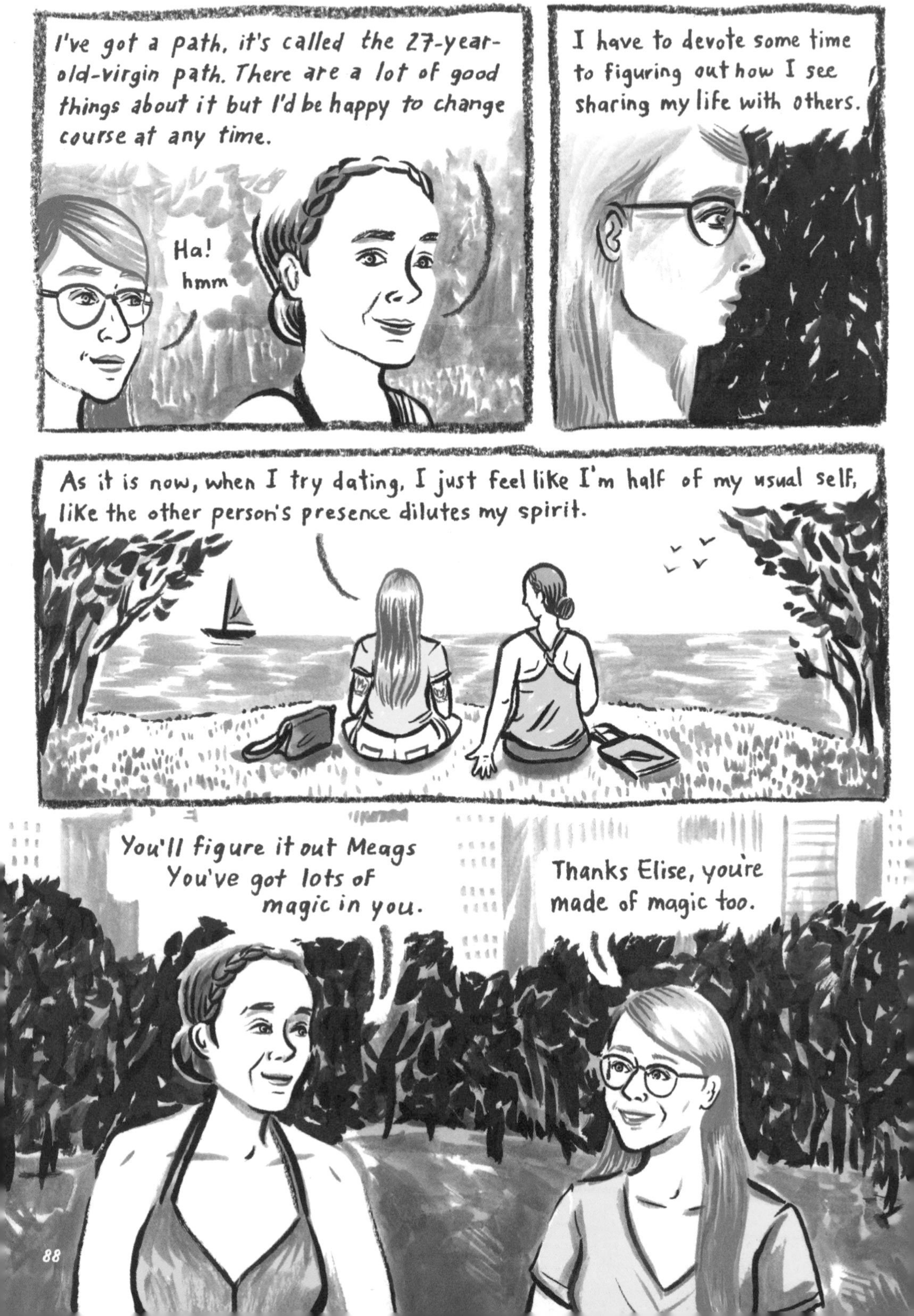
I've got a path, it's called the 27-year-old-virgin path. There are a lot of good things about it but I'd be happy to change course at any time.
Ha! hmm
I have to devote some time to figuring out how I see sharing my life with others.
As it is now, when I try dating, I just feel like I'm half of my usual self, like the other person's presence dilutes my spirit.
You'll figure it out Meags You've got lots of magic in you.
Thanks Elise, you're made of magic too.

'15

From my teenage perspective,
there was a schism at my core
that couldn't be resolved.
Despite being surrounded by
incredibly supportive people,
society's common and casual
dismissal of fluid female sexuality,
or worse yet, the media's
fetishization of bisexual women,
made me feel insecure about
my orientation.

The more time I've spent in
this body, the more I've come
to think of my sexuality as being
comprised of two wholes.
There is no division.

The result of spending years focusing
my attention inward is that I've developed
many of the traits that I would hope to find
in a partner, subsequently becoming my own ideal.

One day, I think I would be happy
to be attached but if it never happens,
I know I enjoy my own company.

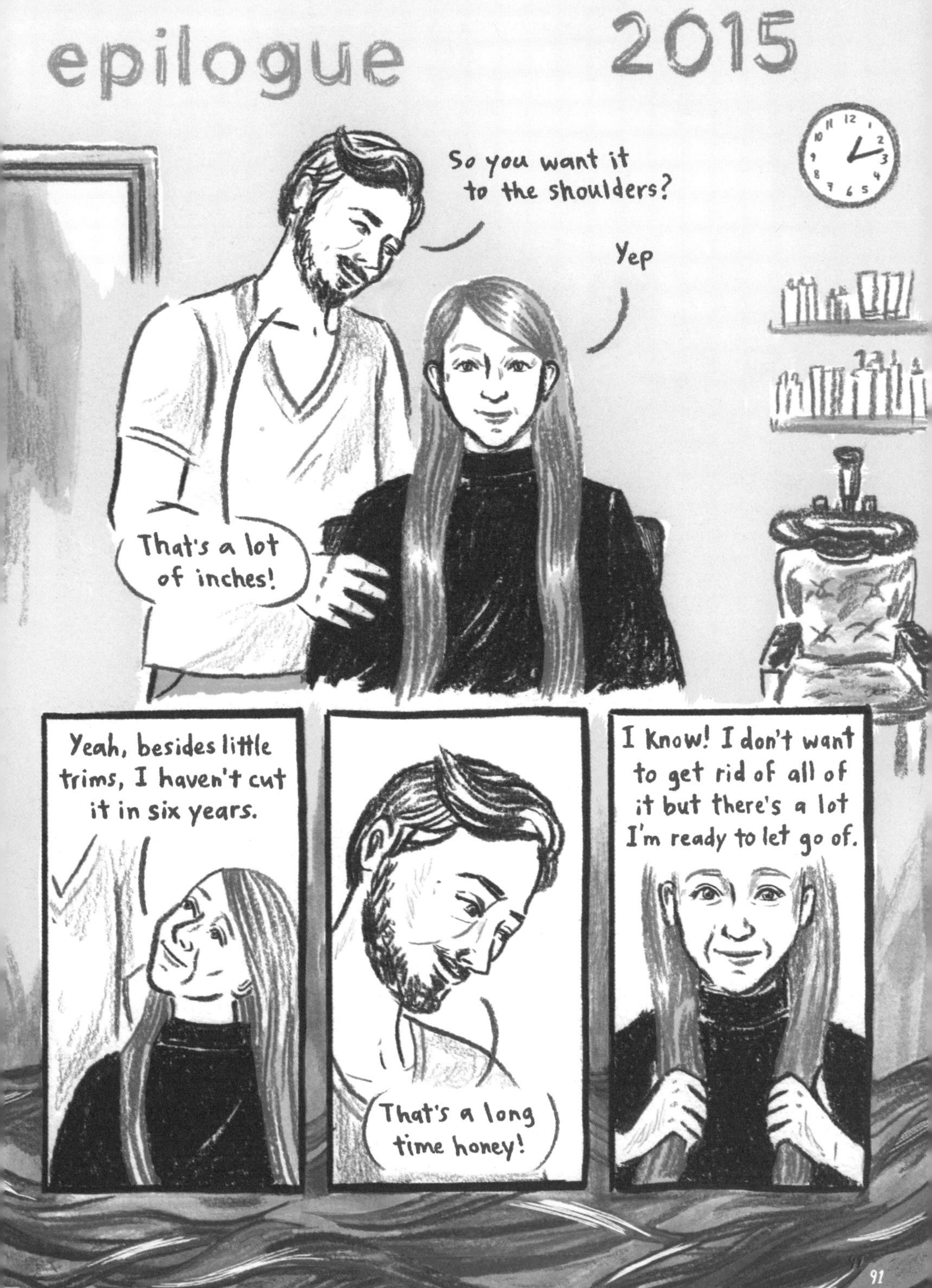

epilogue 2015
So you want it to the shoulders?
Yep
That's a lot of inches!
Yeah, besides little trims, I haven't cut it in six years.
That's a long time honey!
I know! I don't want to get rid of all of it but there's a lot I'm ready to let go of.

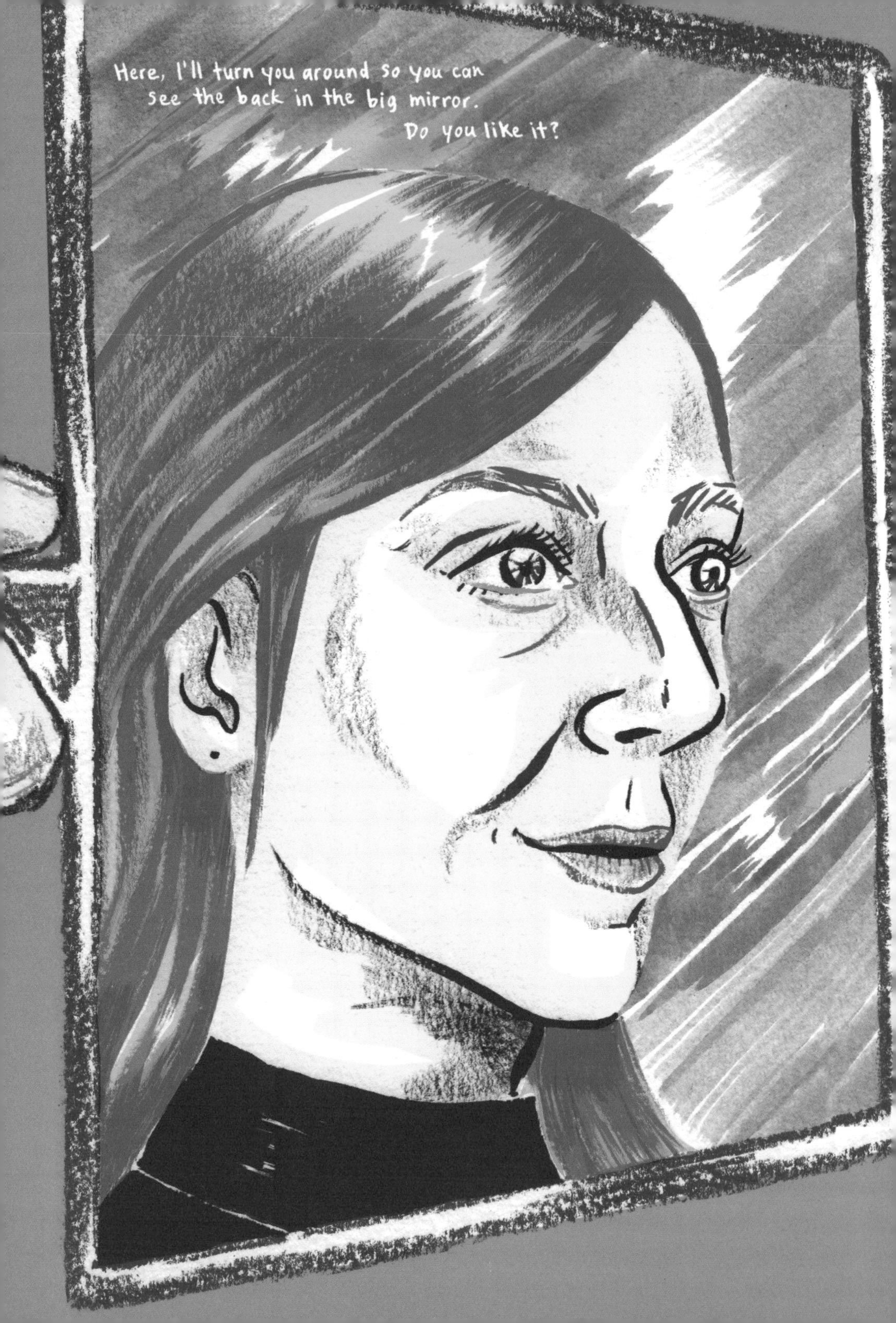
Here, I'll turn you around so you can see the back in the big mirror.
Do you like it?

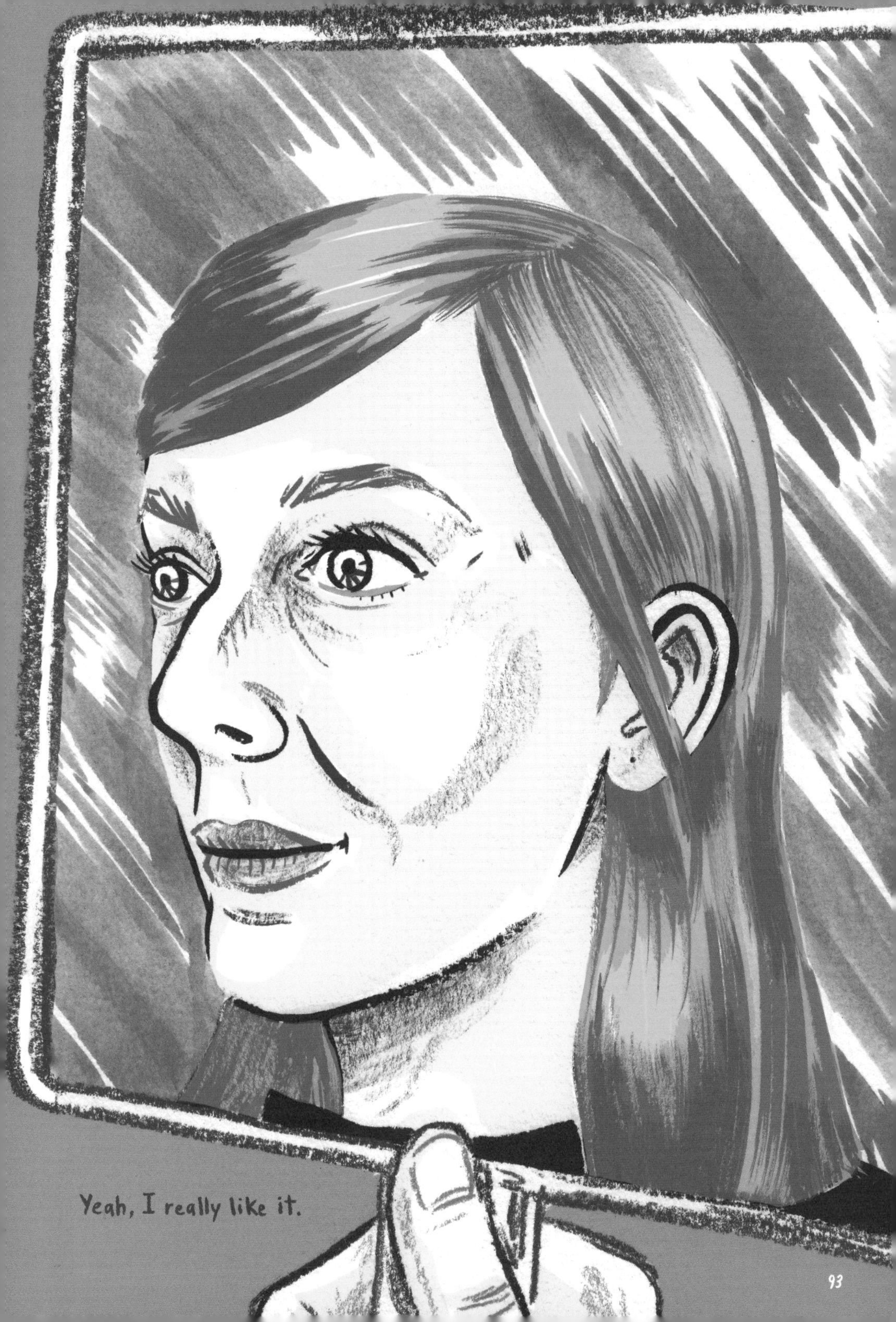
Yeah, I really like it.

notes

I've used the term bisexual in this book, as it was the only term like it that I knew as a teenager, and therefore, the one I most closely identified with. At the time of this publication, many people prefer other terms that have a more inclusive nature, such as pansexual. Personally, I simply identify as queer.

This book is not intended to be a definitive source on bisexual youth. It offers just a few moments of one individual's unique experiences.

These stories were written with the approval of my family and of my friend, known as Elise in this book. The names and likenesses of all other individuals have been changed.

Special thanks to Krista Leger and Georgia Webber for their support.

films & television referenced

p. 7-11 - *Who Framed Roger Rabbit*. (1998). Touchstone Pictures.

p. 39 - *Sabrina the Teenage Witch*. Season 1. (96-97) American Broadcasting Company.

p. 40 - *Buffy the Vampire Slayer*. Season 3. (98-99). The WB.

p. 40 - *Charmed*. Season 1. (98-99). The WB.

p. 41 - *The Princess Bride*. (1987). Act III Communications.

p. 43 - *Labyrinth*. (1986). Henson Associates, Lucasfilm.

p. 44 - *Addams Family Values*. (1993). Paramount Pictures.

p. 45 - *Beetlejuice*. (1988). The Geffen Company.

p. 46 - *Edward Scissorhands*. (1990). Twentieth Century Fox.

p. 46 - *Hocus Pocus*. (1993). Walt Disney Pictures.

p. 70 - *Buffy the Vampire Slayer*. Season 5. (01-02). The WB.

books referenced

p. 31 - Sprenger, J., & Kramer, H. (1487/1971). *The Malleus Maleficarum* (M. Summers. Trans.). Mineola, NY: Dover Publications.

p. 36-37 - Rice, A. (1995). *Memnoch the Devil: The Vampire Chronicles*. Toronto, ON: Alfred A Knopf Canada.

p. 56 - Abbott, E. (1999). *A History of Celibacy*. Cambridge, MA: Da Capo Press.

p. 84 - Easton, D., & Hardy, J.W. (1997). *The Ethical Slut: A Practical Guide to Polyamory, Open Relationships & Other Adventures*. Berkeley, CA: Celestial Arts.

p. 84-85 - Ryan, C., & Jethá, C. (2010). *Sex at Dawn: The Prehistoric Origins of Modern Sexuality*. New York City, NY: Harper Collins Publishing.

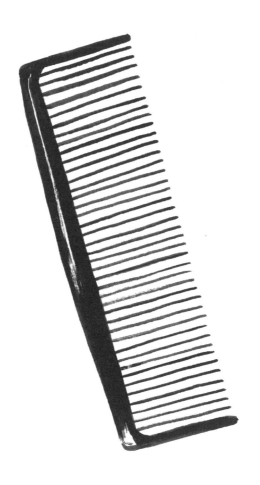